EPIC LIFE

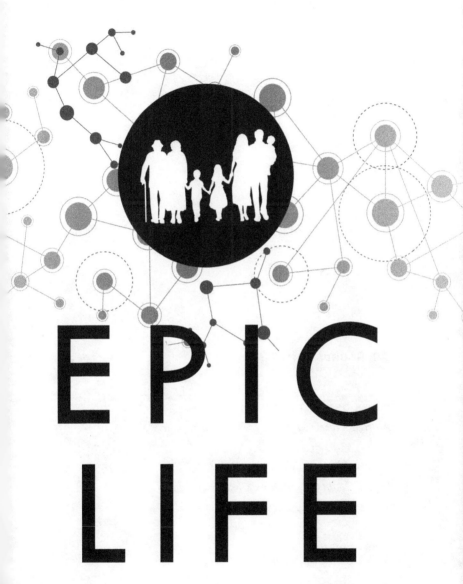

EPIC
LIFE

How to Build Collaborative Global Companies
While Putting Your Loved Ones First

JUSTIN BREEN

HOUNDSTOOTH PRESS

EPIC LIFE
How to Build Collaborative Global Companies
While Putting Your Loved Ones First

FIRST EDITION

ISBN   978-1-5445-3256-1   *Hardcover*
       978-1-5445-3255-4   *Paperback*
       978-1-5445-3254-7   *Ebook*

To my wife, who has taught me how to love
and given me the ability to fly.

CONTENTS

FOREWORD

—PETER H. DIAMANDIS, M.D.
FOUNDER & EXECUTIVE CHAIRMAN AT XPRIZE
EXECUTIVE FOUNDER, SINGULARITY UNIVERSITY

When I wrote my newest book, *Life Force*, with Tony Robbins and Robert Hariri, MD/PhD, I wanted to create a guide that shared the newest breakthroughs in health technology to help maximize readers' energy and strength, plus extend their lifespans.

The purpose behind my book, *Bold*, was, as President Bill Clinton noted, building "a visionary roadmap for people who believe they can change the world—and invaluable advice about bringing together the partners and technologies to help them do it."

With my book, *Abundance*, and global summit and mastermind program, Abundance 360, I have strived to provide mindsets and technologies to allow humanity to rise and create abundance for ourselves and the world.

I first met Justin Breen in Abundance 360 and immediately noticed that he had a particular ability to introduce exponential numbers of other entrepreneurs to the community. Many of the visionaries he connected to the program also joined, creating more and more abundance and connectivity.

Even though we have never met in person (due to the incredible versatility and convenience of our digital world), Justin and I have become great collaborators, as you will see in the following pages and in how he created his newest company through discussions first hatched in Abundance 360.

Justin and I also share the fundamental belief that this is only the beginning of a great and abundant future. This is truly the most extraordinary time ever to be alive.

PROLOGUE

In five-plus years as an entrepreneur, I have had only five truly game-changing ideas.

About one a year.

The previous four were starting my first company, BrEpic Communications; going on a date with my wife once every week in 2018; creating a second company, BrEpic Network; and writing my first book, *Epic Business*.

Scribing this book is the fifth.

There are thirty-four CliftonStrengths, and I rank thirty-second in Ideation—almost dead last. Even the idea for this book came from someone else. Thank you, Bill Bloom.

Almost 100 percent of the ideas that lead my life evolve from the conversations I have with the world's top entrepreneurs. And while I am almost nonexistent in idea generation, I am incredibly aware of when an amazing idea is presented to me as my top three CliftonStrengths are Activator, Maximizer, and Achiever. So result, result, result, result, result.

That is what this book represents—thirty transformational ideas that have been presented to me throughout my life and how I incorporated and activated them into being a husband, dad, and leader of two global companies that only partner with the world's greatest entrepreneurs—or those who will do whatever it takes to become part of that first, elite group.

I started cobbling this list of ideas together shortly after my first book was released in May of 2020. I have written down about thirty—each is a chapter in the following pages—in the two-plus years since. Only the greatest of the greatest ideas—the purest, shiniest nuggets—are included. They represent the best measures of why I have been able to craft what I consider a successful life and role as a visionary entrepreneur.

My entrepreneurial journey started on February 10, 2017, when I had my salary as a journalist cut in half. I could not find a job, so, with zero business background, I decided to incorporate and launch my first company, BrEpic Communications, on April 16, 2017. Over the next six weeks, while I worked full time at half the salary, I reached out to five thousand-plus contacts to find my first five clients. I acquired my fifth client on June 1, resigned from my job on June 2, and renowned media columnist, Robert Feder, announced BrEpic's arrival on June 5, 2017.

The road since has not been easy, but it has been the greatest experience of my life. It has made me feel alive in every way imaginable. The greatest by-product is that I see my wife and two young sons more than I ever could have thought—while teaching my children not only that this entrepreneurial world exists, but that it is possible to create a dream life for yourself and your family.

I hope you take the knowledge in the following pages to simplify your life and that you activate its teachings. Each chapter will conclude with simplified takeaways to help you think and take action.

The roadmap to an Epic Life awaits.

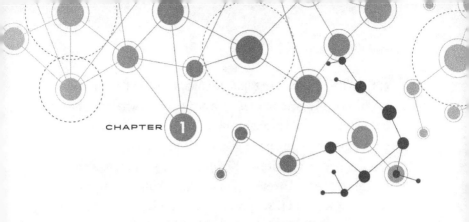

CHAPTER 1

THE CREAM RISES TO THE TOP

Wherever life takes me, I will never stop striving to honor my father, Myer "Mike" Breen, whose favorite expression was "The cream rises to the top."

He was sixty-one when I was born and thirty-four years older than my mom. They met after a drunk driver hit my father's car head-on. The drunk driver was killed instantly. My dad broke most of the bones in his body, but he survived because that is just how my dad was. My mom was his nurse. She wanted him to date her mom, but he wanted to date my mom because that is just how my dad was.

To understand me and my endless drive, you must first understand my parents. They have more hustle than anyone I have ever met, and most of my day is spent talking to the top entrepreneurs on earth who exhibit endless hustle.

My father came from nothing. His parents escaped the pogroms of Russia and settled in Elgin, Illinois, about an hour northwest of Chicago. My grandfather—we do not know what year he was born, but he would probably be around 150 years old if he were alive now—was an entrepreneurial tailor at a small shop on State Street in downtown Elgin. My dad's family, his parents, and his three brothers lived in the same building. My dad was born in 1916, lived through the Spanish Flu, World War I, the Depression, and many other battles that those enjoying creature comforts nowadays cannot even fathom. He and his three brothers all served actively in World War II. His family was featured in national publications for sending all four siblings to war, and for how much they loved their country.

I have no real need for material goods. Most days, I wear the same shirt and do not like fancy things other than nice meals. If our house were burning down, all I would really care about is my family and saving the greatest gift in my possession—my father's war diary from the Battle of the Hürtgen Forest on the Germany–Belgium border.

I am a pretty decent writer, but my dad's diary composed during one of the war's deadliest battles is one of the finest chronicles I have ever read. It is magnificent, capturing the war's tragedy, triumph, blood, guts, struggles, pure agony, comradery, passion, and zest to just survive.

One day, I will have the full diary published, but I have included a few excerpts here, including one written on a Christmas Day (please note it is incredibly graphic and disturbing). Some of the words are indecipherable as my father's handwriting, like mine, was incredibly poor.

NOVEMBER 9, 1944

This is it. All that has gone before, the training, the studying, the discomforts, the irritations take a back seat now.

From now on it's the pay off. Here starts the distinction between the petty discomforts of training and the extreme and acute sufferings of actual war; the griping delays of a problem and the endless boredom of being out in the middle of hell with no one to be with and no one to talk to for hours on end. Here is where you find out what it really means to be miserable, to be so damn cold, wet and hungry that you just don't give a damn about anything.

But there are (unknown word). You are amongst REAL MEN. You see them fight, kill, get wounded and get killed. You see competent men giving all they've got and a helluva lot more, and you're one of them.

CHRISTMAS DAY, 1944

We are in a dogfight between three Mustangs and a F.W. 190 (Nazi plane). The Kraut shoots down two of the Mustangs but the 3rd gets him. We can see him jump but his chute doesn't open. He hits the ground like a ton of bricks about 100 yards from us. The ground is frozen, so when he hits he bounces up about 3 feet and then drops back. Every bone in his body is broken. He's like a mass of jelly.

Some of the G.I.s walk over and cut away portions of his parachute for souvenirs. One G.I. looks at his identification card and papers, which show he was a Staff Sgt., 19 years old, and was flying his first mission.

Well he got 2 for 1 if that's any consolation for him.

JANUARY 10, 1945

A heavy snow had fallen and blanketed the field with about a 6 in. depth of snow. It was very cold and all in all pretty bad flying weather.

We knew that we needed a registration so we sent the group 6×6 up to the strip and told the driver to drive up and down the length of the field several times to beat a path in the snow so we could take off. The truck tires packed the snow down fairly well and made a good path for Walt to take off. It was 3 P.M. when they finally got it completed. We warmed up the ship for 10 minutes and then climbed in without parachutes because we knew that the takeoff would be difficult enough without the added weight of the chutes.

We started at the far end of the runway and Walt got the plane off O.K. and started climbing straight away. He had carb heat on because of the intense cold.

We reached 100 ft. and I called into By (?) to check in. Suddenly the motor went dead!!

Straight ahead, and to the left were forest and hills. We couldn't turn back to get into the field because of lack of power and altitude. The only hope was a slight clearing on a slope to the right. It was a small, very small open field surrounded on 3 sides by high trees. At the far end was a stone barn.

In all the clearing was not over 200 ft. long and 50 ft. wide.

Walt made a 90° right turn as gradually as he could while putting the plane into a glide. The field was not long enough to come in on a normal glide immediately after clearing the treetops Walt gave it right stick and left rudder slipped it in sharply. There was no question but what we would we would crash so I braced myself by grabbing the 2 overhead braces.

He pulled the stick all the way back and dropped the ship in from about 3 ft.; we bounced, hit again, bounced, hit, skidded to the left and came to a stop facing uphill not more than 15 ft. from the stone barn.

My father would return to the United States, fight in the Korean War, and serve as an attorney in Nazi war crime trials. Eventually he became president of an insurance company. Later in life, he was the greatest father to me, my older half-sister, and my two younger brothers.

I had about eight conscious years with him—from age five to thirteen—and he would routinely say, "The cream rises to the top...The cream rises to the top...The cream rises to the top." At the time, I did not fully understand what he meant. He died just before I started high school, and it took me decades to process those six words.

But I started to put the pieces together as a professional journalist during the fifteen years it took to reach my goal of working at a Chicago publication. It fully formed after my salary was cut on February 10, 2017, and after a few weeks of unsuccessfully trying to find a full-time job, and creating my first company, BrEpic, on April 16, 2017. When reaching out to five thousand-plus people to find my first five clients—while I was still working full time as a journalist at about half the salary—those words "The cream rises to the top" never stopped resonating.

If my father, who was shot down numerous times in combat—many times without a parachute—could get back into that plane, I would never stop trying to get to the top of the entrepreneur world, despite having exactly zero business background or training.

The stories of my father and where I come from strike a chord with other top entrepreneurs. Like me, they will do what it takes to manifest greatness in their lives and their companies. They never make excuses. They only make investments. As my entrepreneurial journey has evolved, the only people I partner with now are the ones like my dad—the cream that has risen to the top...or the ones who will make the investment to reach their Everests.

EPIC TAKEAWAYS

Partner with those who will make the investment.

Find strength in your family's history and what you can learn from it.

Are you someone who makes excuses, or will you execute on getting the job done?

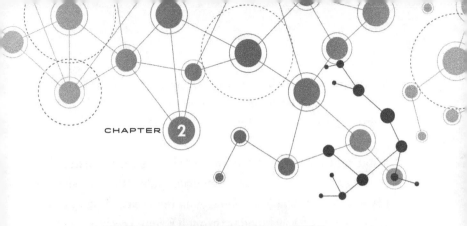

CHAPTER 2

THE PERFECTION
OF PATTERNS

I used to think my greatest skillset was simplifying ideas and activities into stories for my PR firm's clients.

Turns out I was dead wrong.

As the five-year journey of an entrepreneur has evolved, I have realized that my true gift is simplifying complexity in the world into easy-to-understand patterns. More importantly, once I see those patterns, I immediately activate them into my life and my companies.

The most crucial pattern I have seen is this: *Having the right mindset creates the right network, which creates the right opportunities for you.*

I have not done outbound sales or gimmicks in years. I just build my mindset every day—my companies only partner with visionaries who live in abundance and look at things as investments, not costs—which attracts other leaders with the right mindset. At this level, there is no competition. We only collaborate and create opportunities for each other.

What that means in the simplest terms is I am constantly introducing visionary entrepreneurial leaders to other visionary entrepreneurial leaders—around ten great, life-changing intros per day, every Monday through Friday. I receive around two to three every day. Some of those intros lead to more collaborations and partnerships. It just creates more and more abundance. It is limitless.

OTHER PATTERNS I HAVE SEEN AND ACTIVATED:

- Directness weeds out nonsense and magnetizes greatness.
- Confidence attracts confidence and repels arrogance.
- Entrepreneurs care about creating value and purpose; business owners care about bottom line and revenues.
- I am a dad who happens to be an entrepreneur, not an entrepreneur who happens to be a dad.
- I do not sell anything. I am just the buyer. Companies, entrepreneurs, and businesses pay my firms, but I am only buying the people and brands with which I want to associate.
- Give to give, but only to the people who get it.
- The formula for creating a successful global company is surprisingly simple: See a problem; create a solution to the problem; problem solved; successful global company.

There are great practices, tools, and tests I have used to further simplify these patterns.

The first thing I do every day—and I mean every day—is write a Grateful Journal entry to my wife, Sarah. The most important thing for her is when someone tells her, "Thank you." For me, it is not essential, but honoring her is critical. That is why I start my day by writing gratitudes that express the many great things she did in the previous twenty-four hours. You will read more about this later with some specific examples.

For about the last twenty years, I have run outside six days a week, no matter the weather conditions—taking Sundays off. We live in the Chicago area, so it gets cold, hot, wet, windy, and all sorts of ugly climates, but that does not affect me. When I am running between three to five miles, I listen to mindset and motivational podcasts that fuel my brain with positivity and abundance. While listening, I harness those lessons and incorporate them into my life.

Five days a week, I scribe a Grateful Journal entry on LinkedIn. Most of my day, besides hanging out with my family, is spent talking to the world's top entrepreneurs, and the Grateful Journal entry is my way of honoring them.

In short, when you are constantly grateful, it is really hard to be ungrateful. And great practices become great habits.

The three best test resources I employ almost religiously in my life are: Kolbe A Index, Gallup/CliftonStrengths, and the PRINT test.

Kolbe has been the ultimate simplifier. It has four scores—Fact Finder, Follow Thru, Quick Start and Implementor (in this case, Implementor is how you use your hands in a physical way). There are no bad scores, but 1 is the lowest and 10 is the highest.

Almost all of my partnerships are with high–Quick Start, low–Follow Thru entrepreneurs. They are true visionaries, but they need simplification in their messaging and connections. I am the incredibly rare entrepreneur who has high Fact Finder, high Quick Start and high Follow Thru. My 8-6-7-1 is a unicorn score. I talk to a lot of 3-3-9-3s.

For what it is worth, I have also found that my Quick Start score of 7 is the dividing line between folks who make decisions quickly and those who overthink without actually acting. In five years as an entrepreneur, I have only partnered with one person with a Quick Start score below 7—of those whose Kolbe scores I know—and you will read about him later in the book.

Gallup's CliftonStrengths Assessment evaluates thirty-four strengths. Most of the people I talk to are a mix of Ideation/Futuristic blended with Activator/Maximizer/Achiever. They are off in future-land but will do something about it now (i.e., making an investment to activate their future in the present). I am almost dead last in Ideation—32 out of 34—and low in Futuristic. But when I hear a good idea, my top three are Activator/Maximizer/Achiever—so result/result/result.

For me, it is all about taking others' ideas and simplifying them, and then immediately activating those ideas to the world through media or direct intros—many times a combination of both.

Many have heard of Kolbe and CliftonStrengths, but PRINT is far less known. PRINT reveals your unconscious motivators—people see the tip of the iceberg, but they do not see the majority of the massive chunk of ice under the water—your underlying motivators. My score is 8/3. The 8 is to be strong and self-reliant; the 3 is to succeed and achieve. What that means is I do not overthink or over-feel anything unconsciously. I act. Most of the people with whom I partner have similar scores.

Here is how I took all of these concepts into BrEpic Network with my partner, Mark Fujiwara.

With Kolbe, I am 8-6-7-1. Mark is 1-5-9-6. It is perfectly collaborative as my high Fact Finder complements Mark's low Fact Finder. His high Implementor score replaces my miniscule one—I still do not know how to hold a pencil right, and I struggle with building things that even children can easily do. Mark is a genius at building things, including the backstage parts of our company.

With CliftonStrengths, I am Activator/Maximizer/Achiever. Mark is Competition/Maximizer/Empathy. I am dead last—34 out of 34—in Empathy. He is my Collaborative Empathy. And because he is Competition/Maximizer at 1–2, he is going to win and win big at the highest level...with empathy!

With PRINT, I am 8/3 and Mark is 3/8. We are unconsciously motivated essentially the same way. Consciously we complement each other; unconsciously we share our motivations.

When Mark and I convene every week, we always talk about how easy building our platform has been. It is because our skillsets and brains fit perfectly with each other's.

When you can find these patterns and the right collaborators through tests and data, everything seems to take care of itself.

It is not a struggle; in fact, it is a joy. Easy and fun.

EPIC TAKEAWAYS

See the patterns in your life and then activate them.

Kolbe, CliftonStrengths, and PRINT are great ways to simplify your life.

Find collaborative partners who add value to your strengths and replace your weaknesses.

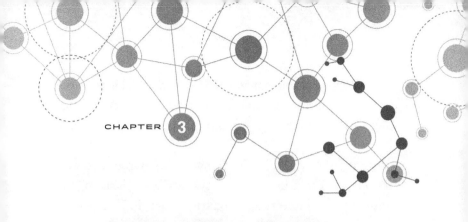

CHAPTER 3

FIND YOUR BABS
OR HAVE YOUR
BABS FIND YOU

Dan Sullivan is the co-founder of Strategic Coach®, a global entrepreneurial group I have been blessed to be a part of for the last few years.

I can confidently say he is one of the greatest entrepreneurial coaches—if not the greatest—who has lived, as he has guided tens of thousands of the brightest, most successful leaders in the world in his decades of coaching.

Dan always stresses that the most important day of his life was when he met Babs Smith, who became his wife and the co-founder of Strategic Coach. Babs is the backstage genius behind Strategic Coach. She built the company while Dan did the coaching. It is a perfect match.

The purpose of my life is "to be a connecting superhero for

every visionary, abundance, investment mindset entrepreneur and share their stories with the world." I am either hanging out with my family or living in that purpose. It is very simple.

With my PR firm, it is easy to live in the purpose of my life every day. There is no extra work besides writing, pitching stories, and connecting visionaries. I love it. It is easy. It is simple. It is lucrative. It is my purpose. I actually "work" zero hours a week.

But when I thought of creating a platform or tech company—the BrEpic Network—I knew there was absolutely zero chance I could do it on my own. Think Dean Wormer in *Animal House*: "Mr. Blutarsky: zero point zero" chance. I would blow up the company. I had to "find my Babs"—the person who could build the business while I talked about it and connected fellow connectors while sharing their stories with the world.

For a few months, in late 2020, I tried to "find my Babs" by myself. I talked about it in meetings. I discussed that concept in media interviews. In fact, I thought I had found the right person, but he wanted to own the entire business and then lease the product to me. That is not a good—or the right—partnership. Remember: I am the buyer.

Peter Diamandis, who wrote the foreword for this book, leads a global entrepreneurial group called Abundance 360. At the level I am at—and I do not care about revenue at all—most of the people in the room are running or have founded $10 million to $10 billion companies. I like to be in a room like that because those are the Ideator–Futurists who will activate now to change the world.

The 2021 Abundance 360 held early in the year was virtual. During the multiday event, I saw that Dan Sullivan was present on Zoom. I started a side chat first thanking him for changing my life through Strategic Coach. I then messaged him that I was "trying to find my Babs." Not sure if he would respond, I was overjoyed to see that he wrote back immediately with a sentence that would impact me forever: "The trick," he wrote, "is to have your Babs find you."

Strategic Coach has many tools that help entrepreneurs determine what they want and what measurements are vital for those outcomes to happen. I think the best one is the Impact Filter®. Essentially, it lists the best and worst possible outcomes and a few "success criteria" that must take place for the best possible outcome to occur. I filled out an Impact Filter, entitled it "Find My Babs," and listed those criteria. After a few days, I started strategically sending it out to a few close friends and fellow entrepreneurs.

One of them was Mark Fujiwara, whom I had never met in person—we originally met in a Zoom room in Strategic Coach—but we had developed an immediate bond because we had the same mindset. Again, if you have the right mindset, it creates the right network and the right opportunities.

I sent him the Impact Filter, and he immediately wrote back: "Let's do this!"

The next day, we had a phone call, quickly talked it over, and laughingly, I told him: "Wow, you are my Babs!"

Mark and I have a full fifty-fifty partnership. I have a simple vision for the company, and Mark executes that vision—plus, he brings his own massive vision for the backstage of the company. I tell him all the time that I would electrocute myself if I tried to do any of the things he has mastered. And he loves that I am the face of the company who draws members into the network.

Mark is based in San Francisco. I live near Chicago. As of this writing, we have only met one time in person—in a late summer launch party held in 2021 at Chicago Yacht Club. Our partnership is the ultimate example of how to create a global company in the era of COVID.

Finding your Babs will make all the difference in your life and business...it is even better when Babs finds you.

EPIC TAKEAWAYS

If you know what you want, the perfect partners will find you.

Do not be afraid to talk about your vision and share it with trusted collaborators.

Building an entrepreneurial company requires the right complementary partnerships.

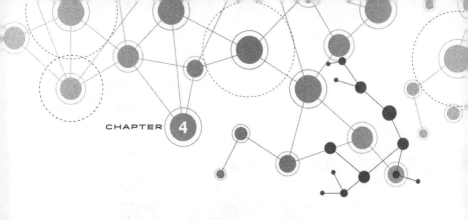

CHAPTER 4

WINNING THE WRONG GAME

Over twenty-plus years as a journalist and more than five as an entrepreneur, I have talked to some really, really bright people.

Jesse Elder is among the most brilliant. We have had many conversations in the past in which Elder provided two, truly key insights. One was that he noticed that key religious leaders such as Moses all shared a key distinction: before they had evolved, they had enjoyed extended periods of stillness, silence, and solitude.

The other distinction occurred when I was mentioning to him that I had been speaking with many entrepreneurs who led conversations with the revenues of their companies, the new car they were driving, or expanding their employee count.

"They're winning the wrong game," Elder said.

The sentence struck me like a lightning bolt. For years, I had been wondering why so many business leaders were focused on surface-level items like revenue, costs, and bottom-line agendas, or showing off with material gains on social media. I have never cared about any of that stuff. I would be perfectly fine living in a cave, well off the beaten path.

Many times, when I meet someone and they open with the material things surfacing in their lives, it is followed by them talking about struggles with their families or never having a family at all. Real relationships are being replaced by material goods and gains.

Unfortunately, I have at least one conversation a week with an entrepreneur who has let entrepreneur life destroy their family life or prevent them from ever having a family.

I am not, and never will be, that person.

Every single day, I ask myself only two questions that truly matter:

1. Did I have at least one good experience with my family today?
2. Did my network grow on a global level?

That is the only game that matters to me. Over the last several years, I have found that the answer to those questions has been yes every day. Everything else has taken care of itself and been the by-product of placing those two questions first and foremost.

To me, that is winning the *right* game with my rules.

And since it is my game, I can win it every day.

EPIC TAKEAWAYS

Play your own game with your own rules.

Do not let entrepreneur life destroy family life.

List the things that really matter to you and win at those.

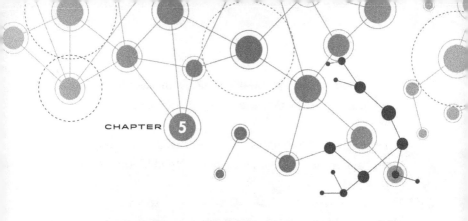

CHAPTER 5

NAME YOUR YEARS

Names represent power and identity.

My wife is a far superior parent to me in every way and makes the call on all important decisions. But when it came to choosing our sons' first names, each child had to have the right one. Those were the only two times in our marriage when I had the final say. Actually, there have been four times because I also named our two dogs, Dr. Pepper (a bernedoodle) and Toffee Kisses (a goldendoodle).

A name signifies honor and a foundation. Roots. A story.

A friend and collaborator, Joe Martin, took naming to the next level by "naming his years." In a TEDx Talk, he described the action as bringing his future self into the present by giving each year an identity. He started the practice in 2014 and has not stopped since.

In late 2019, he told me about the ritual and what it has led to, including starting and selling businesses. That's when I decided to incorporate the discipline in 2020.

I named 2020 "Global Growth." Every day, starting January 1, I said out loud—and in my head—"global growth" at least ten times a day.

"global growth...global growth...global growth...global growth... global growth...global growth...global growth...global growth... global growth...global growth..."

At the start of 2020, my PR firm included only domestic partners, and almost all of my conversations were centered in the United States. I began that year with a trip to a client in Salt Lake City—remember this was just before COVID shut things down—and I really wanted to expand my audience beyond the country's borders as I knew my firm's process could benefit anyone, anywhere.

As the year evolved—and COVID certainly fast-tracked this—I began having far more virtual discussions around the world. The three groups with which I spend a great deal of time—Strategic Coach, Abundance 360, and Entrepreneurs' Organization—feature members across the world. With people locked down, it opened up endless opportunities to collaborate on a global level. I started speaking with visionaries in Canada, South Africa, New Zealand, Australia, Japan, Thailand, Mexico, England, Germany, France, Israel, Costa Rica, Brazil, Pakistan, Northern Ireland, Ireland, Saudi Arabia, United Arab Emirates...even Bhutan and Luxembourg. Some partnered with my firm.

The daily practice of uttering "global growth" had led to...global growth.

I began to see that there truly were no limits in life, so at the end of 2020, I decided that 2021 would be the year of "No Limits."

Again, every day, I would say "no limits" out loud or to myself. *When you have no limits, there are no limits.* If I felt during a certain day that I was limiting myself, I would remember that 2021 was "No Limits." It was a great way of limiting my limitations.

"No Limits" to me means starting a new company with a partner I had never met in person until throwing a giant launch party at Chicago Yacht Club in late summer.

"No Limits" represents raising my PR firm's investment rates to levels that I never would have thought possible. By the way, raising rates attracts serious, investment-mindset people who live abundantly and with no limits themselves.

"No Limits" allows me to have the mindset to continue to make bigger and bigger investments in my family, myself, and my network—and in the rooms where I want to be. Bigger investments lead to smaller rooms, but the people in those rooms are making bigger impacts.

I keep investing more and more to be in the right spaces—where the entrepreneurs in those spaces are making the most impact. And some of those entrepreneurs make huge investments with my companies, which helps them make huge impacts in the world through media and connections. That enables me to spend as much time in the smallest room possible—my home with my family—where I can make the most impact.

"No Limits" comes full circle.

I was discussing the "naming your years" practice during a podcast interview with friend and collaborator, Bill Bloom, in the summer of 2021. He asked me what I would call 2022. Because I am so low in Ideation, I told him that I had no clue yet, but I hoped eventually it would come to me.

He then noted that maybe I could label 2022 "Epic Life," as my first book had been called *Epic Business*. Moreover, I was continuing to spend more and more time with my family while building my first company and starting a second that was collaborative with the first.

In that discussion, Bill not only gave me the name of the year but the very title of this book.

Epic Life, to me, represents family first, creating greatness for your network and yourself, and shedding material niceties for real relationships and value. Truly living and giving with the purpose of giving to the people who get it.

It is epic...or nothing.

Naming your years is a transformational practice. It can power your mindset and simplify your focus for a full calendar year—and far beyond.

EPIC TAKEAWAYS

Naming your years represents power and identity.

What would you name your current year and the next one?

Writing things down and saying them out loud allows them to manifest.

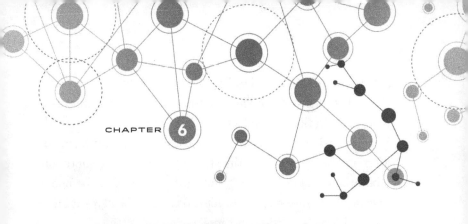

CHAPTER 6

THE MORE YOU SEE WHO, NOT HOW®, THE MORE YOU'LL SEE YOU DIDN'T SEE

Like any good journalist, I try to know to whom I am talking before an introductory meeting.

In the least, if they know it or have taken it, I ask people for their Kolbe scores. Again, it is the ultimate simplifier for understanding how people will act—or whether they probably won't activate at all.

I have collaborated with only one person (that I know of) who had less than a 7 Quick Start, and that exception is Jayson Lowe. Based in Western Canada, he is a truly global thinker and doer. A 5 Quick Start, he acts much more like a 9 or 10. He owns and runs multiple, successful companies, growing them exponentially with team members—seemingly by the quarter.

After we were introduced by Richard Canfield, who is a 9 Quick Start, Jayson heard what my PR firm did and signed later that day. No hesitation. He understood that my first company could be an immediate gain for his various businesses, creating intro after intro after intro, and thus leading to potentially more collaborations that he told me "would last a lifetime." Remember: give to give to the people who get it. Jayson is 100 percent fully one of those visionaries who gets it.

Jayson has provided endless value to me as well, from him and Richard interviewing me on their podcast, to dishing out oodles of verbal golden nuggets. His best came during a Strategic Coach session in late 2021, when Jayson said, "The more you see who, not how, the more you'll see you didn't see."

Jayson was referencing Dan Sullivan and Dr. Ben Hardy's first mainstream book, *Who Not How*®—one of the best and most important pieces of literature I have ever read. Essentially, if you are not truly world class at something, find someone else who is better at it to do it for you—or have them find you.

I am among the best in the world at connecting abundant, investment-mindset visionaries and creating simple-to-understand stories that the media loves highlighting. That is not arrogance—arrogant people think they are great at everything—but supreme confidence. I know the value that my PR firm and connecting platform provide far exceed the investment levels. The rates to join my two companies weed out all nickel-and-dime thinkers and businesses and only attract the world's top entrepreneurs or the ones who will make the investment to become part of that first group.

Other than those two abilities—and being a good husband and dad—I am basically useless to society. Things a trained monkey can do would drive me bonkers. And I am OK with that.

If I do not absolutely love doing something—and I mean truly have passion for it—I do not do it, or else I have someone else (or technology) do it for me.

With the PR company, I have a team of freelance reporters—really great ones—who write many of the stories. I have a person who frequently updates the website; a financial advisor and accountant who makes sure taxes are paid on time; and a slew of partners that if a service does not fit into my sweet spot, I just send the opportunities to them. I spend essentially 100 percent of my day either with my family or focusing on connecting and collaborating with other leaders throughout the world. Scheduling is run through Calendly and other platforms. I control my time and when I want to talk to people.

With BrEpic Network, Mark Fujiwara runs everything behind the scenes. He found the collaborator, David Mansilla—you will read more about him later—to build the platform. Mark and his team provide the logistical support to onboard new members. And Mark absolutely loves being backstage in his zone of genius. I just talk about the company during events, media opportunities, and one-on-one discussions. When people are interested, I introduce them to Mark and his team for the onboarding process. It is like Joe Montana passing to Jerry Rice, who effortlessly runs into the end zone for a touchdown, and the whole team celebrates.

So many business owners are plagued with trying to do too many things—or everything—themselves. My Kolbe score of 8-6-7-I has literally been defined as "I've Got This," so embracing others has been a gradual process. Now I fully understand that "We've Got It" is a million times better than "I've Got It."

And, as Jayson said, the more you see the *who*s in your life, you'll see why you don't have to do many of the *how*s anymore.

EPIC TAKEAWAYS

Focus on what you are truly great at.

It is OK to be world class at only a few tasks.

Others who are much better at things can do those things for you.

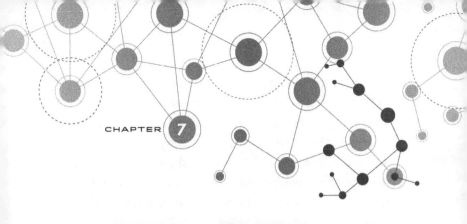

WHAT ARE YOUR CORE VALUES?

Darius Mirshahzadeh has one of the best first paragraphs of any book I have read.

He begins his masterpiece, *The Core Value Equation*, with: "'I hate this company,' I said to myself, sitting in the office in San Francisco. 'I cannot believe I created this.'"

Darius goes on to describe how he built a hugely successful, multimillion-dollar, 150-employee company with his twin brother—and how that business was basically destroying his life.

Having key core values was transformational to Darius's success moving forward. They created, as Darius said, the "ultimate decision-making engine for [his] organization."

Over the years, I have crafted my core values for BrEpic and now BrEpic Network around the same three key words:

Abundance, Visionary, and Investment. I partner only with entrepreneurs who have those three attributes in their mindsets. I have never mapped the actual data, but my guess is that one in one thousand people and just a small percentage of the entrepreneurial population have all three. Many of them have (or at least act like they have) Abundance and are Visionaries, but when it comes to making the investment, they are halted by their own cost-first mindset.

Even at the start of my entrepreneurial journey when I had zero clients and zero revenue, I looked at everything as an investment, never a cost. The first networking group I joined—and I am still in it because I am loyal to the people who get it—was a $250 annual investment. Some of the groups I am in now cost more than $25,000 each, annually. But again, they are investments, not costs. In the coming years, I will join groups that are $50,000-plus annually because they are even better investments.

I have still never partnered with someone who asks, "What do you charge?" within the first ten minutes of an initial meeting. Those are people living in a transactional, scarcity world, not the transformational, abundance space I inhabit.

The Abundance, Visionary, and Investment values are truly at my core. I can tell right away when someone does not have all three. If they do not, I will not talk to them again unless their mindset shifts. Most of the time, it never does, because they do not and never will "get it."

People ask me all the time how I have built a global network with only the top leaders and visionaries who live in abundance and look at things as investments, not costs.

The simplest of answers and litmus tests is this: *If I talk to someone and I know that they will take time away from me and my family, I will never talk to that person again.* They have disqualified themselves from being in my life or my network—unless their mindset shifts and they are ready to act and make an investment. And I am OK with that because the people who do qualify are the ones who "get it" and will give to give to others who get it. If there are about eight billion people on the planet and I partner with 0.1 percent of them, that is still *eight million people*. They are the ones creating the companies and concepts that employ or are enjoyed by the other 99.9 percent.

It all comes down to the values at my core. They attract the right fits and repel everyone else.

Like Darius's great book, it is an equation: Visionary + Abundance + Investment = Time with My Family and Changing The World. Or $1 + 1 + 1 = \text{Infinity}$

That is the only math that matters to me.

EPIC TAKEAWAYS

What are your core values?

Core values attract the right fits and repel the wrong ones.

Having the correct core values can simplify your life and grow your businesses.

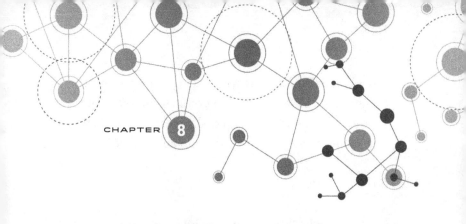

THE JOY OF THE BANK RUN

I am incredibly grateful to be a weekly guest on Scott Becker's business podcast.

Scott is a serial entrepreneur who happens to be a Harvard Law School graduate. He has led law firms and media companies, and his events regularly include speakers such as President Bush, Hillary Clinton, Peyton Manning, and other global leaders.

Yet Scott is always humble and always strives to learn more and more—constant evolution.

During one of our interviews in early 2021, I was driving to my local bank to deposit a check that had been written for my PR firm. That became the basis of our interview, and Scott jokingly said it would be great if my next book included a chapter about the "joy of the bank run."

I told him during the interview that I would do just that, as I thought it would be worth a chapter in terms of the process of making money—what that actually means—and then seeing that money physically deposited into an account.

So here we are.

I incorporated BrEpic on April 16, 2017—six days after I turned forty years old and two months and six days after my journalist's salary had been cut. I could not find another full-time job.

I had absolutely no idea what I was doing, as I had taken zero business classes in college. I did not even know what an LLC or a W-9 was, or that you had to pay taxes four times a year. I still do not know what "S corp." stands for, which I think is funny.

While I was working full time as a journalist at a reduced salary, I reached out to five thousand people to find my firm's first five clients over a six-week span. It was probably more than five thousand, as at the time, I had well over twenty thousand followers on social media built from decades as a journalist— and I sent messages to pretty much all of them. But the five thousand for five clients simplifies things.

One of the first clients was a small Chicago restaurant that is now out of business. Since I was trying anything to make a buck and did not know what I wanted to focus on as an entrepreneur, our contract noted that I would run the restaurant's social media accounts and take photos and videos of the food they were making. This is not my expertise, but I had training as a photographer. I had a decent social media following, so I thought it would be a good fit.

I sat in the restaurant in late spring when the owner signed the paper contract—this was well before I used DocuSign—and printed out a check at his small kitchen with the name BrEpic Communications, LLC and $500 as the payment.

It was the first check I would receive, and despite it being only $500, I was smiling ear to ear.

Later that day, I made a bank run to deposit it.

That $500 check is still the smallest I have ever deposited, but as the payment rates have increased scores of times—my guess is it will be 100 × $500 in the next year or two to engage with my PR firm—I always appreciate and enjoy going to the bank to deposit a check when it is a physical one.

Most of the payments I receive now are electronic or via credit card, but every now and then, a check comes via UPS or through the mail.

The bank is a three-minute drive away, and it is fun to put the check in the ATM and watch it instantaneously show up as "pending" in the account.

When Scott and I talked during the podcast on my way to the bank, he noted that many entrepreneurs do not drive to the bank anymore. I look at the experiences as great reminders of where I came from and where I am now, and then I understand that the checks will only get bigger and bigger as the value my companies provide—and the networks they serve—get greater and greater by the day.

The bank run really is a joyful experience.

EPIC TAKEAWAYS

It is fun to go on the occasional bank run.

Are you raising rates and seeing bigger and bigger checks deposited into your account?

Bank runs are great reminders of the past and where your business or businesses are heading.

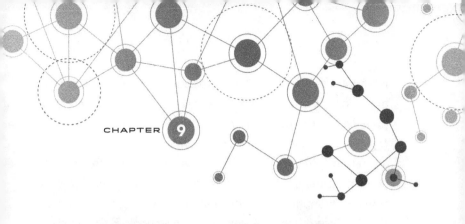

PEOPLE WHO PAY, PAY ATTENTION

Both companies I founded serve only the world's top visionaries—or the ones who will make the investment to become part of that group.

It is a select audience, a minority within a minority. The 0.1 percent.

I have chosen this elite group for two reasons:

- They are really the only people who understand what I am talking about, because people like me are usually aliens within their own families, communities, and verticals.
- The investments they make in my companies allow me to spend more time with my own family.

These are the people who will actually make the investment—or pay—so I pay attention.

Brandon Voss stressed the expression, "People who pay, pay attention" during one of our many conversations. Brandon is president of the Black Swan Group, which trains the world's top companies, leaders, entrepreneurs, and brands in negotiation that leads to results. Black Swan Group was founded in 2008 by Brandon's father, Chris Voss, the former lead international kidnapping negotiator for the FBI. I am also grateful that Chris wrote the foreword for my first book, *Epic Business*.

On my CliftonStrengths, I am dead last in Empathy and second to last in Includer, so it makes sense that BrEpic Network is an invite-only, high-price-point connectivity platform for only the best of the best who will gladly make the investment to become part of this group. They know it is not a cost, but a great investment.

What has been interesting in the process of building BrEpic Network is that a good percentage of the first members were current or former partners of my BrEpic PR firm. They had already "paid" and had been incredibly satisfied with the results of sharing their stories with the world, so they "paid" again to be part of BrEpic Network.

Those are the people I pay attention to. Moreover, when they have recommendations for what they want from BrEpic Network and how it can be better, I listen. Many times I will communicate with Mark Fujiwara to make sure those ideas are integrated into the platform. Remember: all I care about is that it works and that a monkey can use it. What develops from the platform is what users—the people who pay—want.

I think that is the key for any successful entrepreneurial journey moving forward from COVID and the Zoom era: understanding that companies are not really "businesses" but instead they are collaborative platforms where the users determine what they want and the best ways to accomplish their goals. Like my dad getting into a plane many times without a parachute, I am not afraid to build the platform and see what happens.

I know people will pay, because I have seen the success of BrEpic and what will be greater, exponential growth with BrEpic Network.

I love guiding the ship and having so many attentive visionaries on board to share this voyage together as we sail into uncharted entrepreneurial waters.

And I am paying attention to what those payers want.

EPIC TAKEAWAYS

Honor those who make investments in your business or businesses.

What do users want from your products or businesses? Pay attention to their requests.

When people are pleased with results, they will likely become customers of your additional companies.

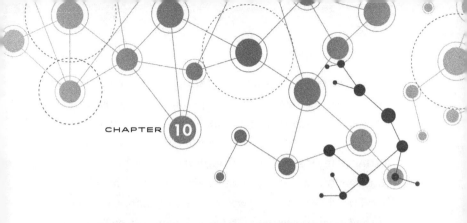

CHAPTER 10

GRATITUDE JOURNAL

My father's last living brother, Stan, was married for seventy years to his bride, Fran.

A few years before Stan died, I was lucky enough to talk to him via phone on my wedding day—May 4, 2008—to ask for marriage advice.

He told me two things:

- Always put my wife, Sarah's, needs before mine.
- Never touch the thermostat.

I said that during my wedding speech, and people laughed, but in the years since, I have really tried not to touch the thermostat unless I am home by myself. I walk past the thermostat and chuckle sometimes because I really do not want to go near it.

I have also used that analogy when thinking about going outside my zone of genius or doing things I do not like to do: *never touch the thermostat*. I just stay in my lane.

I never saw my father cry, and I witnessed Stan tear up only once, when my mom got off the phone with the hospital the evening of January 18, 1991. She told my family, who were sitting at the living room table, that my dad had died. Stan was sitting to my right, and I will never forget how he was the first to say anything. "Let's have a moment of silence," he said before breaking down. I think it weighed on him that he was the last of the Breen brothers—who had miraculously survived wars, depressions, poverty, and so many other obstacles—to live. The last soldier standing.

Besides my father, there is not a man I respect more than my late Uncle Stan. I will admit I am crying right now just writing this sentence because he was such a great human being. When I started as a journalist, I would send him and Fran articles, and they would always write back with encouraging words. In college, he told me to read Machiavelli's *The Prince*—which teaches that truth matters. Always truth. Always results.

The first time he met my wife—we visited him and Fran at their retirement village in Naples, Florida—he walked me to the elevator and said, "Justin, she's a gem. Now you can have a life. Do not f-- it up."

It is the only time I ever heard him swear.

Sarah and I started dating on August 28, 2004—the day before she started medical school. I told her that I loved her on September 4, 2004, because saying it on that first date would have been too fast. So I waited a week.

There is a simple reason how I know there is a higher power

watching over us: without a God, there is no way someone like my wife would ever marry someone like me.

Sarah is the kindest, warmest, most loving, empathetic, caring, and responsible person I have ever met. Pediatricians send their children to see her. She found the perfect calling.

Sarah has given me a life in every way imaginable. I try really, really hard not to f-- it up, though for a visionary wackadoo like me that is not always easy.

That is why I begin every day with the Gratitude Journal to Sarah. I began writing it on October 5, 2020 after talking to an entrepreneur who had been journaling daily for years about his family and what they meant to him. It is really hard for me to say "Thank You" as it is just not natural. But I can write. So, the Gratitude Journal is my way to thank Sarah every day. I am including some examples in case it is helpful for you to start your own journals.

FRIDAY, OCTOBER 16, 2020

It was a delight to watch Sarah smile and laugh during teacher conferences yesterday. The kids are so much like her...Jake is dedicated and brilliant and a leader. Chase so warm, an incredible learner, a joy to be around. Sarah is an amazing doctor, but where she really shines and is in her true element is being a mother and a guide to the children. She cares so much—it can't be quantified. Her heart flows into the children. Such a blessing.

In both my books, the only acknowledgment has been to my wife. Without her, I am lost. I am forever grateful to her. The gratitude for her has shaped the gratefulness in everything else that's wonderful in my life.

Because, when you have that gratitude, it is incredibly hard to not be grateful.

EPIC TAKEAWAYS

If you are constantly grateful, it is hard to be ungrateful.

For whom are you grateful? How do you let them know?

A Gratitude Journal is a great way to honor the ones you love every day.

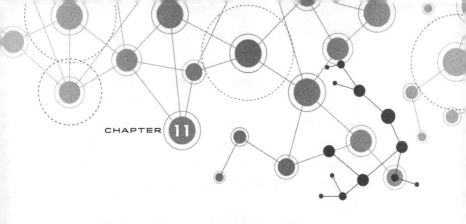

CHAPTER 11

THE CONVERSATION BECOMES THE PRODUCT

Mark Leyden and I have had only one conversation, and it produced this chapter.

Mark is an Indianapolis-based entrepreneur who assists business owners and families, including some members of the *Forbes* 400, in design and funding of wealth transfer and business succession plans. He and I met during a Strategic Coach session, which led to our later talk.

During our Zoom chat, we were talking about BrEpic Network, which at the time was still in the development stage. He noted that: "the conversation becomes the product."

Though our meeting was only about thirty minutes, I have thought a lot about that one line over the last several quarters.

In real time, Mark's and my conversation led to me writing this chapter, which essentially is a product.

With BrEpic Network, I was talking for years that my PR firm BrEpic was not a PR firm at all but really just a "giant incubator of geniuses, and we are constantly introducing each other for mutual gain. The by-product is that I am constantly receiving intros to companies around the world that want to hire my firm." Really, BrEpic PR was just a global network that kept growing by the day.

Even in the foreword for my first book, *Epic Business*, Chris Voss wrote the paragraph: "Like the success of The Black Swan Group—where I used my years of expertise as a negotiator to build a business that created a groundbreaking model that helps businesses and brands everywhere—BrEpic is doing the same thing with its approach to public relations and building real relationships with a *global network.*"

This was written in late 2019, well before I had the idea that I would start another company. But the "network" aspect was already there, right in front of me. Even though it was in writing, it was still part of the conversation—a starting point to talking about what my first company actually is, and how it has evolved with a collaborative second business that is just a connecting platform for what I already was doing with my PR firm.

Basically, every chapter in this book is the product of conversations I have had with other entrepreneurs or discussions I have had through experiences in life. Again, the very title for this book and naming 2022 "Epic Life" came through a podcast interview with Bill Bloom. This book is a collective product of intellectual products, discussions, and mindsets.

That is why I am so open to sharing this knowledge and all the "secret sauces"—even my PR firm's entire process is on the website. There are no tricks. It just solves the problem. Because I am open to sharing the details, it leads to more conversations, which lead to more products, wisdom, and results.

The greatest entrepreneurs do not hide their secrets. From my years of having conversations, they love taking deep dives into their successes and collaborating with others who can complement their skills with their own open-source knowledge.

It will be fun as BrEpic Network evolves over the years to see the conversations, companies, and products that develop from those relationships. Bigger and better futures begin with sharing ideas, and then acting to create a deliverable product.

This chapter is but a small example of the greatness that can come from the shortest of conversations.

EPIC TAKEAWAYS

Be open to feedback when discussing your new ventures.

One conversation can change your life by creating a product.

Collaborating with entrepreneurs through discussions can lead to amazing outcomes.

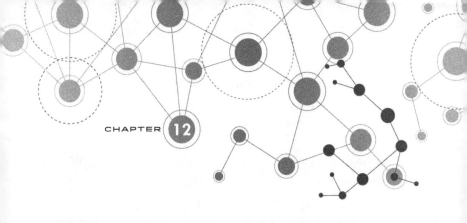

CHAPTER 12

ARE YOU AN ALLEY CAT?

Bob Saget was one of the funniest people who ever lived.

I think the most hilarious thing about him was that he played this all-American TV character on *America's Funniest Home Videos* and *Full House*, but he actually was one of the dirtiest, raunchiest, sadistic comedians of all time. He had zero filter. I mean, really, really sick stuff.

Truly epic.

The day after Saget died, I listened to a podcast interview he gave with fellow comedian, Marc Maron, about embedding in that industry for decades. They both said that comedians had to be insane to want to be comedians. And Saget stressed that they were like alley cats roaming the back alleys in the dark hours, while the rest of the normal world was fast asleep in their safe abodes.

Entrepreneurs are alley cats too. Most people would never put themselves through what every entrepreneur certainly endures to start a business, let alone scale it or launch another one. Like alley cats, entrepreneurs thrive and find their bounty when no one else is looking.

Entrepreneurs are like comedians with fewer jokes. We are like a legalized version of the mafia—I love the part of *Goodfellas* where Ray Liotta and his date go through the club's side entrance and kitchen before getting a front-row table erected for them while the rest of the guests wait in line. Entrepreneurs do not wait in line or conform to society's rules. We make our own rules and play our own games. Like alley cats.

My first journalism job was delivering the *Boulder Daily Camera* in Colorado. The shift started at 1:00 a.m. and usually ended right before sunrise. I saw a lot of actual alley cats and other critters delivering papers—some truly weird people too. My car was stolen once; the thieves got away and hundreds of papers were left in their wake all over the street. I thought that was pretty funny.

Most of my twenty years as a journalist were spent on late-night shifts. Many times, I didn't get home until 2:00 a.m. While the rest of the world slept, we journalists performed to put out a paper or news website.

Alley cats.

Starting my first company, when I had zero revenue and absolutely no business background, I cannot tell you how many nights I was up at 2:00 or 3:00 or 4:00 a.m. strategizing for the next day. That is an entrepreneur's life when you're beginning a first business.

I love running right before the sun comes up in our suburban Chicago neighborhood—especially when it is below freezing. It is when I get the greatest focus for the upcoming day, especially when I listen to other alley cats on podcasts and other platforms talk about entrepreneurial life.

Heck, I wrote Chapter 27 of this book at 2:00 a.m. in early February 2022 (let me know how you think it turned out).

I have not met a successful entrepreneur who is not or was not at one time an alley cat. Most people do not achieve the success that entrepreneurs have because they would never take the chances or lurk in the back alleys of life at night. They do not feel comfortable there.

I have found that all entrepreneurs are *most* comfortable in those spaces. Like Bob Saget said, "You have to be a little insane to choose this life, but you also must embrace being an alley cat."

I try to sleep through most nights now, but when I am up in the wee hours, I am never surprised to see an entrepreneur messaging me or to find myself having a brief online talk about the upcoming day.

Once an alley cat, always an alley cat.

EPIC TAKEAWAYS

What are you doing when no one else is looking?

All great entrepreneurs embrace the alley cat mentality.

When starting a company, late-night hours are great times to think and strategize.

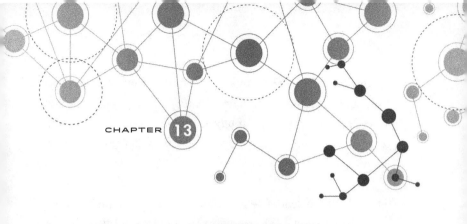

THE PROCESS IS
THE SHORTCUT

Most entrepreneurs at the highest level just want the answer.

They do not care about details.

Less is more.

Simplicity.

Visionary, Nic Peterson, has built a life of creating processes for himself and the six-, seven- and eight-figure businesses he has launched—and for the numerous ones he has helped others scale to unprecedented heights.

During our many conversations, Nic has provided endless, wondrous wisdom, but my favorite expression of his is, "The process is the shortcut."

Every successful entrepreneur I know is a master of at least one great process. Their businesses fit into that same process I see time and time again. *The formula for creating a successful global company is surprisingly simple: See a problem, create a solution to the problem, problem solved, successful global company.*

These brilliant leaders—and their teams—have just created processes to solve the problem. To deliver a solution better, faster, and easier. Or, as the literal definition of "shortcut" states: an accelerated way of doing or achieving something.

My PR firm works—again, the entire four-step process is on BrEpic's website—because it just solves the problem. It is a shortcut at the highest level to obtain massive news coverage and incredible media connections to the right-fit audiences. That is why it is successful for any vertical. The only one I stay away from completely is politics, because it is the opposite of a Visionary, Abundance, Investment mindset.

The process is the shortcut.

With BrEpic Network, entrepreneurs at the tops of their games do not want to spend time interacting with the wrong-fit individuals for years only to realize they are bad fits. They just want the right intro from the right person. Problem solved. Successful global company. They will gladly make the investment to become part of the Network because it is a great shortcut to activating the right relationships better, faster, and easier.

It is the same process to solving the problem.

Any company will achieve more greatness by simplifying their processes that create better and faster solutions.

Processes are the keys to opening endless doors of shortcut opportunities.

EPIC TAKEAWAYS

Less is more.

Great entrepreneurs always look for shortcuts.

What processes can you simplify in your company or companies?

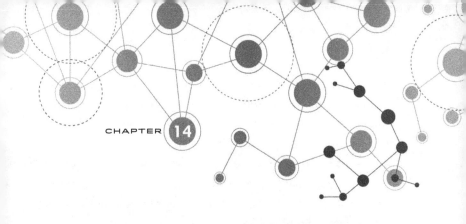

CHAPTER 14

CLEAR THE MECHANISM

As far as movies go, *For Love of the Game* starring Kevin Costner is, at best, two stars.

But there is a four-star moment for an entrepreneur near the beginning of the 1999 film, where Costner, in his last time on the mound as Detroit Tigers starting pitcher Billy Chapel, throws a perfect game against the New York Yankees in the Bronx.

As fans heckle him, horns blare, and New York City subways rattle in the background before his very first pitch in the first inning, Costner says a simple line to himself in his head: *Clear the mechanism.*

After he says those three words, everything goes silent and out of focus, except Costner's clear-as-day view of his Tigers catcher and opposing Yankees batter.

It is my favorite scene in any movie, which is surprising because the actual film is not that good.

Supreme concentration, like Costner had on the mound, is critical for any entrepreneur. No doubt most people will not understand you when you are starting a business. Most of society will be like the fans in the stands trying to distract you—not because they are bad but because they will never grasp the idea that your goal is to hit the outside corner at the knees with a pitch that can catapult your life and business to ultra-great heights.

My whole existence is about clearing the mechanism with my mindset and actions. If I am not with my family, friends, or embedded in the purpose of my life—"to be a connecting superhero for every visionary, abundance, investment mindset entrepreneur and share their stories with the world"—I do not stray. I do not go out of focus.

Like an ace pitcher before fifty thousand fans, the great leaders and CEOs are not afraid to go out on the rubber and perform at the highest levels. Regardless of what is said by detractors and onlookers, there is a result to be had. A focus to get there. A goal that must be achieved.

At the time of the first pitch, the only people who matter to Costner are his catcher and the Yankees batter. That is how I feel about my family, partners, collaborators, and network.

Everything else is out of the arena and cannot distract me from the elements that shape my life.

Clear...the...mechanism.

EPIC TAKEAWAYS

Focus is critical for an entrepreneur's success.

How do you "Clear the mechanism" in your life?

Be wary of outside forces that are distracting you from your main goals.

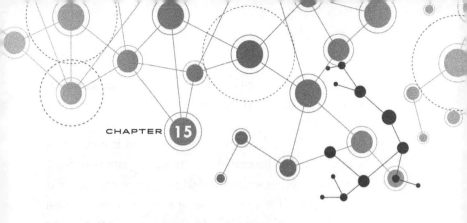

CHAPTER 15

GODWINKS

I stopped believing in randomness years ago.

My wife and I were meant to meet a few days after my grandmother died.

My salary was supposed to get cut so I could begin this entrepreneurial journey.

Joining Strategic Coach, Abundance 360, and other groups was not random. It was part of the bigger plan to guide me to writing this chapter...right now.

A few examples:

Strategic Coach has events called "taster days" where prospective new members hear from panelists—entrepreneurs who have been in the program with great success for many years. One of the panelists on the taster day I attended—it was in person then—was Bill Bloom. At the end of the session, I pulled out my laptop and started checking email. But as he walked by, I stopped working to thank him.

We talked for a few minutes and agreed to meet in a month or so. We would wind up becoming best friends, starting a podcast collaboration together with artificial intelligence entrepreneur Evan Ryan, and Bill would become a BrEpic PR client. As a member of Chicago Yacht Club, Bill was also able to sponsor the BrEpic Network launch party event I held there.

After my first book was released, entrepreneur Mike Malatesta asked me to be on his show. Mike, who has been through more adversity and setbacks than almost any entrepreneur I have ever met and has helped start, grow, and sell two eight-figure companies (I strongly recommend reading his book *Owner Shift*), had heard me on another podcast and was intrigued.

At the time, I would always say, "Abundance mentality is the only mentality." During our interview, I said that, and he mentioned he was part of a group called "Abundance 360" that would be a perfect fit for me. A few months later, I joined.

Mike would become a BrEpic PR client as well, and Abundance 360 is where I would plant the seeds of BrEpic Network, and where I would meet Peter Diamandis, who wrote the foreword for this book.

Nothing random about any of that.

In summer 2021, I had a great conversation with Teresa Easler, who leads a Toronto-based business that helps corporations and individuals become exceptional communicators. Teresa, who is also an associate coach in Strategic Coach, is an exceptional communicator—friendly and direct, which is easier said than done.

When we talked, I mentioned how all these amazing events happened in my life, and that they were not random.

"I call those 'Godwinks,'" Teresa said.

Exceptional communication right there.

"Godwinks" is a perfect term to replace "not random."

The daily advancements in science and technology are beyond incredible. Recently, I met an entrepreneur in the metaverse, and while we were talking in a virtual room, we started messaging on LinkedIn, where we scheduled a time to convene again on Zoom by using Calendly to schedule the event. Think about that. It is incredible!

But as technology gets faster and faster—microchips get smaller and smaller—there are two constants that will never change: (1) the power of storytelling and (2) the power of real relationships.

I know those meetings and those real relationships are not random. For me and for most of the global entrepreneurs I speak with daily, having "Godwinks" in our lives is essential. Appreciating that a higher being is at work and at play—regardless of religion or beliefs—in guiding our way is comforting, transforming, and powerful.

The best entrepreneurs I know would never try to play God; instead, they benefit endlessly from Godwinks.

EPIC TAKEAWAYS

Technology cannot replace real relationships.

Godwinks create amazing events and possibilities.

Are you putting yourself in the right real or virtual rooms?

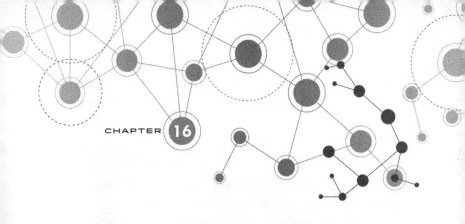

CHAPTER 16

BE A SMALL GIANT

I rarely meet someone with a similar Kolbe score to my 8-6-7-1.

Steven Neuner is one of those unicorns. A former president of the board of directors for Entrepreneurs' Organization Dallas, a current member of YPO Dallas, and an associate coach within Strategic Coach, Steven has been an entrepreneur since starting a lawn-mowing company as a teenager. He is also a 5-6-8-1 Kolbe, meaning he has a slightly higher Quick Start than I do—8 to my 7—with the same 6 Follow Thru.

When we first talked a few years ago, I told Steven that I had met only a handful of entrepreneurs with Kolbe scores close to mine. It is rare air as most of the people I talk to are at least a 7 Quick Start with 3-or-less Follow Thru. Thus, they almost certainly must hire people to follow through for them. Otherwise, nothing will get done. When I tell them my Kolbe score for the first time, they usually stare in silence for a few seconds because they cannot fathom how my brain works and activates.

Steven has been an entrepreneur much longer than I have, and he dropped two nugget bombs during our initial meeting.

One was that people like Steven and me are "hit the gas, pump the brakes" entrepreneurs. Meaning, we "say it, do it"…"say it, do it"…"say it, do it." Things do not get forgotten or handed off to a plethora of people. They are just executed.

Two other words he spoke were transformational when he described us as "small giants." Entrepreneurs with high Quick Start and high Follow Thru, he said, tend to be masters in only a few areas, but they go as big as they can in those fields. They do not stray beyond what they truly care about. They think and act globally, but if it is not in their wheelhouse, the brakes kick in and keep them on the track.

Small giants.

Being a small giant is a giant gift. While others are measuring revenue, employee count, office space, number of cars and houses, and other material items, I measure time with family and my global network. The by-product of focusing on family and building real relationships is I have not done outbound sales in years. I just magnetize the people I want in my network, create value for them, and they create value for me and the others in my network.

I keep doubling down on the same two things: family and network. I am continually getting better and better at spending time with family while providing more and more value to my network. That includes raising rates in the process, because that just increases the quality of the entrepreneurs who want to be involved and will make the investment to become part of the select group.

Small giants do not get distracted by distractions or potential ones. We are focused on a few things—I have not met small giants who are fixated on more than three or four focal points. We just want to be giants in our own small spaces, where we can make the most impact. More focus leads to more impact, which leads to even more focus, which creates even more impact. It is the orb that never stops expanding or providing greatness and value.

I know I am lucky to have an 8-6-7-1 Kolbe. It allows me to easily change the world in my own special ways.

But I think any entrepreneur can be a small giant if they find their calling. It is just a matter of whether they can install their own brakes or utilize a company of employees to provide the brakes and boundaries for them.

EPIC TAKEAWAYS

In what areas are you a small giant?

Any entrepreneur can change the world in their own ways.

Doubling down on your talents creates endless value for you and your network.

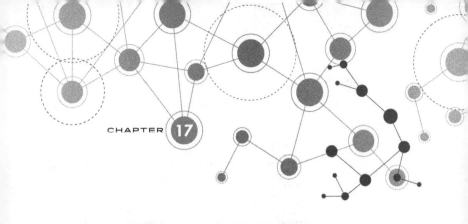

CHAPTER 17

AVOID BORING PEOPLE...AND AVOID BORING PEOPLE

Boring as an adjective means "not interesting, tedious, and causing weariness and restlessness through lack of interest."

As a transitive verb, bore is defined as making "someone feel impatient or dissatisfied, especially by talking to them about things that are not very interesting."

The next three chapters are focused on the people who are not in my network and why that is. I am writing these not to be rude, but to truly try to help the audience determine whether they are in the wrong rooms with the wrong networks—with tips to avoid being in those places with those folks.

Remember on my thirty-four CliftonStrengths, I am dead last in Empathy and second-to-last in Includer. So, it has been easier for me than most to exclude wrong-fit people from my companies and attract the select few who get it. That does not mean I do not sympathize with people, but that is much different from empathizing with their circumstances, because I know what it takes—without exception—to make it to the highest level of entrepreneurship. There are no excuses here—only executing and making the investment.

As I have continued to make bigger and bigger investments to join smaller and smaller rooms, I have found that the percentage of boring people continues to exponentially drop. The entrepreneurs in the best rooms are the least boring people on the planet. They are changing the world through new technologies, companies, tools, concepts, organizations, foundations, and partnerships. They are also finding great joy in transforming ideas into true breakthroughs with action and investment. They are not bored, they are not boring, and they are not boring anyone else in the room with their revolutionary companies.

If I am not in the right room, I become bored almost immediately. It has been like that my whole life because I have always been surrounded by truly amazing people. That started with my dad when I was a kid, to then writing stories about the coolest people on earth as a journalist, to now promoting, highlighting, and connecting the world's greatest entrepreneurs through media and platforms.

Anything besides doing that and spending time with my family, to me, causes "weariness and restlessness through lack of interest." I am *so bored.*

And when I interact with fellow visionaries, I am very aware of not boring them, because I know they are almost certainly like me and do not want to be bored with uninteresting topics. I get right to the point and quickly say what I am up to; from great projects like this book, to starting a second company with a partner who is anything but boring; to having massive media publications promote what I am up to.

I am constantly stimulated when interacting with geniuses who are not boring. It is endlessly thrilling to be part of these networks and know that not only do I belong but I can genuinely help others with my own exciting initiatives.

Boredom is the opposite of energy—the inverse of excitement.

If you are bored, surrounded by people who bore you, or you seem to be boring others, maybe it is time to find a room that fuels instead of drains you.

EPIC TAKEAWAYS

Do not bore people and avoid those who bore you.

You will never be bored if you are in the right rooms with the right people.

Are the people in your life boring you, or are they giving you energy?

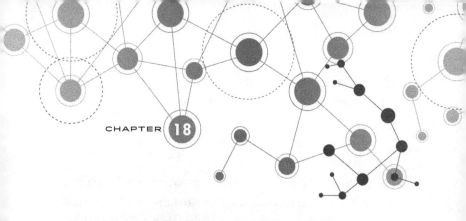

CHAPTER 18

TIME VAMPIRES—STAY AWAY FROM THEM

Nothing annoys me more than people who talk endlessly without taking action.

I call these people "time vampires"—they suck the life out of me and waste my valuable time.

In five-plus years as a full-out Activator entrepreneur, my biggest struggle has been how I handle my reactions to time vampires and how I have evolved from learning how some people just happen to be talkers who have no intention of backing up their words with investment.

This simplifies it best: Talkers are takers. The biggest talkers, many times, are the biggest takers. They love sharing how great they are without the ability to appreciate to whom they are talking. They relish in receiving essentially what comes down to free consulting.

As an entrepreneur, I have compiled a list of how a potential time vampire acts with some warning signs:

1. If someone sounds too good to be true, they are almost certainly too good to be true.
2. If they ask for endless advice or your contacts before committing to an investment, they are likely wasting your time.
3. If you ask how a time vampire is doing and thirty minutes later the time vampire on the other end is finished with their answer, they are a time vampire.
4. If after several meetings, they decide to concoct gimmicks to try and pay for your services, they are a time vampire.
5. If they are more than five minutes late to a meeting and do not apologize, they are a time vampire.
6. If someone asks, "What do you charge?" within the first five to ten minutes of an initial conversation instead of "What does an investment with you and your firm look like?"...they are a time vampire.

My favorite time vampire story was when an entrepreneur met with me at least five times. This person told me every time how great he was, and he even asked me to allow him to give a speech at one of my client appreciation events. I let him, even though his company was not a client.

I had not learned about true time vampires at that point. His speech was truly bizarre. It had nothing to do with my company or business. The guests were genuinely confused. A few weeks later, I asked him if he ever planned to invest in my company to share his story with the world. He said he did not have the funds. Time vampire.

Another time vampire called me out of the blue after I liked one of his Facebook posts. I had never met him, and I have no idea how he got my number. He said he was building a new company and would love my firm's help. He brought me into meeting after meeting after meeting, promising everyone in that room—there were well over a dozen entrepreneurs in each meeting—that he was going to hire my firm. Three months later, he asked if I could take equity in the company instead of a direct payment as he did not have the funds to pay my firm. No thanks, time vampire.

I have always been direct—really direct—but I am beyond direct at this point because I have learned so much about time vampires. Remember that my entire litmus test is: *if I talk to someone and I know that they will take time away from me and my family, I will never talk to that person again.* It really simplifies things and how I take action.

I am glad I have been through those experiences with time vampires because I can spot them more easily now. If someone talks endlessly the first time I meet them, I just send them what a partnership agreement looks like. If they sign, great; I gave them a mulligan.

If not, they are done wasting my time.

I hope this helps you avoid making the same mistakes I have experienced. The time vampires are out there. Do not let them prey on you.

EPIC TAKEAWAYS

Time vampires talk but do not take action.

Time vampires are easy to spot if you look for the right clues.

Do you want to spend your life with people who talk but do not make the investment?

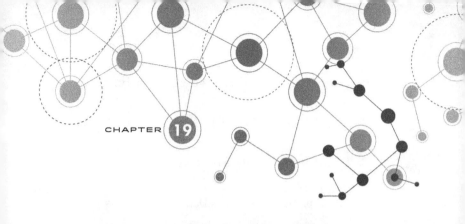

CHAPTER **19**

MEDIOCRE PEOPLE DON'T LIKE HIGH ACHIEVERS, AND HIGH ACHIEVERS DON'T LIKE MEDIOCRE PEOPLE

On December 5, 2021, I posted the following message on my social media platforms about the greatest current coaches with their ages as of that date.

> Manager who just won the World Series is Brian Snitker. He is 66.

> Best coach in women's college basketball is Geno Auriemma. He is 67.

> Best coach in the NFL is Bill Belichick. He is 69.

Best coach in college football is Nick Saban. He is 70.

Best coach in pro basketball is Gregg Popovich. He is 72.

Best coach in men's college basketball is Coach K. He is 74.

Best entrepreneurial coach is Dan Sullivan. He is 77.

Respect your elders. Appreciate greatness in coaches and their wisdom learned over time.

I will focus this chapter on Nick Saban, the head coach at the University of Alabama and the current record holder for the number of college football national championships with seven. His teams seem to be in the College Football Playoff, which features the top four teams in the nation every season. Considering there are 130 Division I teams that can hypothetically make the final four every season, basically knowing the Crimson Tide will be one of them is truly mind-boggling.

Saban has given many amazing motivational speeches, but my favorite is from 2019 when he told a group of Alabama supporters why his teams had such great chemistry.

"It is because," Saban said, "mediocre people don't like high achievers, and high achievers don't like mediocre people." If everybody doesn't buy into the same high standard you have as an organization, you're never going to be successful," Saban added.

Saban went on to stress that his entire point of spring practice—college football is played in the fall and winter for those who do not know—was to eliminate players and coaches who did not belong on the team bus. He wanted to weed out the mediocrity.

Remember: there are no excuses at the highest level, only investment. Regardless of whether you are part of the best college football program in the nation or want to partner with the world's greatest entrepreneurs, there is no time for an excuse.

Because the cream rises to the top.

I do not understand people who aim to be second rate. I have just kept raising rates to attract bigger and bigger thinkers and doers. The story that will always stick in my mind is when a close family member laughed when I increased my PR firm's minimum rates to $10,000. He could not understand who would make an investment like that. I told him that people with the opposite mindset would gladly do so, as they have continued to do as I have continued to raise the investment rates.

Most of the world is filled with people who will laugh at, or not fathom, what high achievers are trying to do. Why? Because they are not high achievers.

They will watch your entrepreneurial game from afar and ridicule you when things go wrong and perhaps fake cheer when you score big. But they will never want to actually be on the entrepreneurial field and go into battle with you. They do not get it. They will never get it because they do not have the guts or gumption to even strive for the greatness you quest to achieve.

That is why I have surrounded myself with other high

achievers—and by the way, you do not have to be a visionary entrepreneur to be one. My wife is a pediatrician and an incredibly high-level achiever. She does not need to own the business to be a hero to her patients.

In his speech, Saban also mentioned how, when he worked as a defensive coordinator for Bill Belichick from 1991–1994 when Belichick was the Cleveland Browns' head coach, Belichick had one simple sign in the training facility: Do your job.

That is what being a high achiever means to me: doing your job to the absolute best of your ability. And always trying to get better.

Mediocre individuals will never realize what true greatness is—or do what it takes to get there. As you rise, you will see who belongs on your journey and the ones who cannot or will not get on the bus with you.

EPIC TAKEAWAYS

Mediocre people do not like high achievers.

High achievers do not like mediocre people.

Are you doing what it takes to be a high achiever?

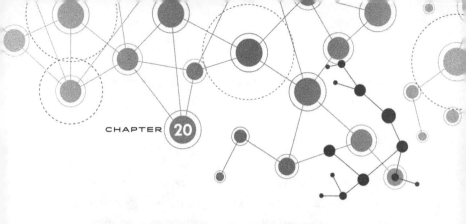

CHAPTER 20

YOU CAN'T CREATE WHEN YOU CHASE TIME

I have spent the last three chapters detailing the three types of people I avoid like the plague: Boring, Mediocre, Vampires.

The best explanation came during a conversation with Dr. Jeff Spencer, who is anything but a boring, mediocre vampire. Dr. Jeff has coached and partnered with leaders like Richard Branson, Tiger Woods, Bono, Lance Armstrong, and Jim Kwik. He is also a former Olympic cyclist himself—realizing a dream he had since he was seven years old. And Dr. Jeff is a 3-8-8-3 Kolbe—he is the only one of three 8–Quick Start, 8–Follow Thru entrepreneurs I have ever met. That is the ultimate hit the gas, pump the brakes—I guess in Dr. Jeff's case, churn the pedals, push the brakes.

He is a master of balance.

During one of our talks, I asked him how he crafted his life of family first and partnering with some of the biggest names and brands on earth. Dr. Jeff said, "You can't create when you chase time."

Jackpot.

I have interacted with so many frustrated entrepreneurs who are stuck chasing the wrong people, leads, opportunities, and activities. They cannot create anything because they have no time to do so.

That is why I eliminate so many wrong-fit people from my life. They would just prevent me from creating experiences with my family and the companies that celebrate right-fit visionaries and help connect them to other like-minded geniuses.

Because I have so much time, I can plan a six-day summer trip where I take my sons to major and minor league baseball games across the Midwest. I can go to Turks and Caicos with my wife for our wedding anniversary and not think about anything else.

I can write this book with an ample amount of energy. I can have global conversations with the most interesting people, and those conversations lead to more and more connectivity and potential products. I can perform at the highest level when serving as a guest on various media platforms, which is great for me and my brands, but also for my PR firm's partners as the show hosts always want to interview them after they talk to me.

The biggest mental battles I hear now are with visionaries who started as entrepreneurs, but they devolved into business owners because they lost the ability to manage their time.

They have become so busy chasing time, meetings, employees, bottom lines, a mortgage, new car payments, and other agendas, that they have lost any potential to create anything new or have any collaborative communication.

By competing for time, they have lost any hope of creative collaboration.

EPIC TAKEAWAYS

Chasing time destroys creativity.

Entrepreneurs embrace having ample free time to create.

How are you chasing time? What activities can you eliminate?

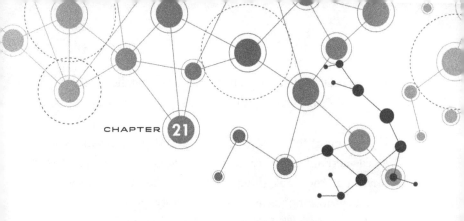

CHAPTER 21

THE ONLY THING YOU CAN DO WRONG IS DO NOTHING

Dave Erickson grew up on a North Dakota farm with a wooden outhouse.

In the years since, he has developed the first widely used payment platform for internet sites. Now he is bringing economic services to the Rising Billion by empowering local groups via "e-commerce in a box" facilities along with the ability to receive and send money to create self-organizing, emergent local solutions to local problems. He describes himself as a full alien, and I think he is right—in a good way. Dave and I met through Abundance 360, where there are a lot of aliens crafting and building out-of-this-world companies, literally.

During our numerous calls over Zoom and smartphones, Dave has expanded my mind to not only think outside the box but literally imagine possibilities outside Earth.

Yet the best guidance he has provided is when he uttered the simple phrase, "The only thing you can do wrong is do nothing."

If you cannot tell already, I love literal definitions and what words actually mean. As a pronoun, *nothing* equates to "not anything," "no single thing." But I will take Dave's expression and use "nothing" as an adjective signifying "having no prospect of progress," "of no value."

To me, people who do nothing with talk and no action provide no value. Business owners who delay with "maybes" and schemes prevent true progress and growth. I much prefer someone who says no because, in that case, it is an active answer. The right no has always led to the right yes.

Even the smallest action is far superior to doing nothing at all. Act to get organized!

It is like fishing. You will never catch anything without a line in the water.

There is no progress with no action, even if that action is saying no. Because that no will lead you to where you want to say yes.

Dave, whose childhood was spent on the wheat farmland of the Dakotas, is living proof of what action can lead to. So are all the other global visionaries I connect with daily.

They know anything is possible because they would never do nothing.

EPIC TAKEAWAYS

Nothing is wrong unless nothing is done.

Saying no is much better than saying maybe.

Are you taking action with your life or standing on the sidelines doing nothing?

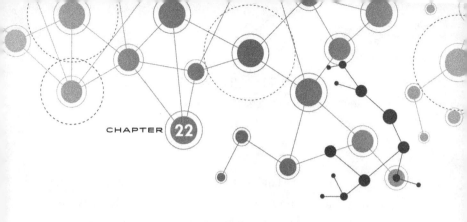

CHAPTER 22

IKIGAI

BrEpic Network co-founder, Mark Fujiwara, is the greatest.

Not only is he a tremendous entrepreneur and a full backstage genius but he lives for purpose and connectivity.

We had an immediate bond, even though our first interaction was during a Strategic Coach side-chat on Zoom. The things we were writing about concerning abundance and global thinking just meshed.

During our first one-on-one, I was talking about a concept I had recently learned and was starting to implement in my life. It was entitled *ikigai*, a Japanese term that was essentially "one's reason for being" or "a lifestyle that strives to balance the spiritual with the practical."

There is also a book about the concept called *Ikigai: The Japanese Secret to a Long and Happy Life* in which the author reveals daily habits of the world's longest-living people.

Before I could finish, Mark discussed his own love of *ikigai* and that he even had an *ikigai* tattoo on his arm!

A Godwink for sure.

Mark is a few years older than me, and some of his children are a bit older than mine. He has partnered with the world's top entrepreneurs for nearly three decades not only to help with their finances but also their health and longevity. Mark is a full-on entrepreneur who happens to be a financial advisor—the exact opposite of the typical bean counter in his world.

He has been in the game of life and entrepreneurship longer than I have with more wisdom and greater experience.

I value that tremendously. I learned from him how to live in my *ikigai* at all times. If my thoughts or actions do not fit into my *ikigai*, they need to be eliminated.

Mark also has a tattoo featuring the saying *ichigo ichie* on his body. That term means that every meeting represents a once-in-a-lifetime opportunity and to treat it as such. It is a powerful add-on to *ikigai*—live for your reason for being, combined with balance and understanding that every day and every event is a chance to capture true greatness.

I feel blessed every day that I am alive, to be with my family, to find more and more purpose, and to collaborate with greater and greater visionaries.

Ikigai and *ichigo ichie* are there waiting to be found, appreciated, and activated.

EPIC TAKEAWAYS

Finding balance is the key to achieving more balance.

Do you implement *ikigai* and *ichigo ichie* into your life?

Treat every opportunity like it is a once-in-a-lifetime moment.

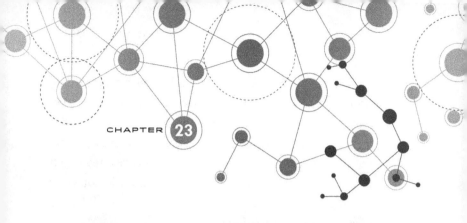

CHAPTER 23

LEAD WITH YOUR HEART

On March 11, 2020, Utah Jazz center, Rudy Gobert, tested positive for COVID, and the NBA suspended its season.

That was the moment when COVID became real for me and, I think, for many other Americans too.

In the almost two years since—I am writing this chapter on February 8, 2022, which would be my dad's 106th birthday if he were alive—I have done exactly two in-person meetings strictly related to my companies.

One was for the great BrEpic Network launch party held at Chicago Yacht Club in late summer 2021 where we had entrepreneurs from around the world, an awesome band, and luckily, beautiful midwestern weather. That is still the only time I have met my partner, Mark Fujiwara.

The only other business meeting not on a computer or smartphone was with Aidan Uttinger, a truly special human being and entrepreneur who grew up in New Zealand but is the definition of global. A BrEpic PR partner, Uttinger was traveling the world in the fall of 2021 and asked to meet in person when he was in Chicago. We talked for an hour, most of it about finding purpose in life and following that purpose, and toward the end of the conversation, Uttinger told me he was heading to O'Hare Airport the next day with no clear intention of where he would go next, because he had many options with friends in a multitude of destinations.

I asked how he would choose, and Uttinger said, "I will lead with my heart. That's how I make all my big decisions." Then he pointed to his heart.

Uttinger has had numerous successful companies. His latest is literally The Love App—a platform designed to spread love around the world to those who need it most. Users globally can earn cryptocurrency Love Coins by sending their heart's energy wherever it is most needed. A user simply requests love and then people all around the world opt in; their apps sync together; and everyone sends a focused two-minute, guided, love meditation directly to the recipient.

Uttinger has built a company based on love by leading with his heart. During our conversation, we talked about how his previous ventures were fun and lucrative, but they did not provide purpose or passion. He was pouring everything into The Love App because, he said, it is what his heart told him to do.

In the weeks and months that followed our meeting, I thought a great deal about leading with my heart and how it related to action. My heart is focused on family and network. It's a true passion for creating experiences with my family and transformational value for the global visionaries with whom I interact.

What has been really interesting is every partner or collaborator within the BrEpic family shares the same mindset of changing the world. There is a much higher purpose to their goals beyond financial gain. They have built businesses to solve major problems or raise awareness of global issues.

I think it starts with them leading with their hearts. The body's engine guides the decision to build their companies...and their brands' missions are to make the world better while creating fuel for their hearts.

It's a perfect heart–energy circle.

EPIC TAKEAWAYS

Choosing passion has lifelong value.

Your heart can be a great decision-maker.

Are your biggest choices based on making money or creating purpose?

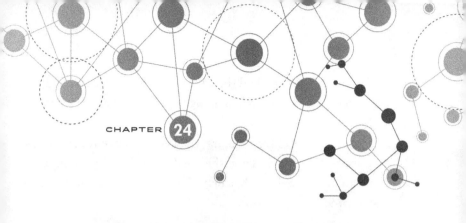

CHAPTER 24

UNCERTAINTY IS AN OPPORTUNITY TO COLLABORATE

A few days after COVID started to shut down the United States, I posted on social media that the event would be the greatest opportunity of all time for those with the right mindset.

While I sympathize with how COVID has affected so many families and businesses—my wife had COVID in winter 2020 and was quarantined in our bedroom for ten-plus days while I watched our sons—the pandemic has created endless abundance for those who can see and leverage those opportunities.

A BrEpic partner in 2020, Missing Link, was based in South Africa. Before COVID, they were Africa's largest, in-person public speaking tutorial company. It was pretty tough to do that during COVID. So, Missing Link quickly pivoted to an all-virtual platform. They taught speakers how to monetize their appearances and had their best quarters ever in Q2 and Q3 of that year with BrEpic helping to promote their services.

I know numerous entrepreneurs who lost 100 percent of their revenue in a few days. Then they just flipped the script and came up with something better within their company, or they just started another one.

The formula for this success was simplified during a Strategic Coach Zoom session in summer 2021, when entrepreneur Alan Olsen said, "Uncertainty is an opportunity to collaborate."

Alan is managing partner at GROCO, one of the top CPA firms in the United States, where he partners with some of the most successful venture capitalists and entrepreneurs in the world. He is also one of the most connected people I know, and that is saying something. He interviews many luminaries on his weekly *American Dreams* show that has aired since 2011.

He has led GROCO since 1990, and he certainly has seen a great deal of uncertainty in the decades since.

COVID created the most uncertainty in human history. My guess is we will never see another period with this much uncertainty in our lifetimes.

Overall, I have found it incredibly exciting. Because I have the right mindset, I realized instantaneously that COVID was an opportunity to leverage technology that would replace traditional travel for meetings. I could see my family more. Heck, I could even start a new venture with someone I have met only once in person. I could think globally because everyone was on the same page in their same rooms at home.

COVID was the great reset button.

While I am guessing most of the world was engrossed with negative news and input, the conversations I was having around the globe were focused on what opportunities, products, and collaborations would develop from the shutdown. It was all-out abundance.

Leaders around the world wanted to share their stories with the world, which benefited my PR firm. Entrepreneurs everywhere wanted to connect online, thus opening Zoom platforms for Strategic Coach, Abundance 360, Entrepreneurs' Organization, and endless other networking groups.

It has been the greatest opportunity ever to build real relationships in a digital world. I have never met several of my new best friends; I will probably never actually meet many of them.

That does not mean we cannot collaborate.

The best entrepreneurs like Alan Olsen love times of uncertainty. They have the opportunity to use their brains to their full ability—to solve problems and then execute those solutions themselves or through collaborative teamwork.

Uncertainty for us means certain excitement!

EPIC TAKEAWAYS

Uncertainty equals exciting opportunities.

Collaborations emerge when there are uncertainties.

During uncertain times, are you living in scarcity or abundance?

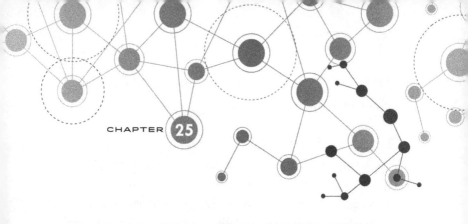

THE OBSERVER CREATES HIS OWN REALITY

As a young father, David Mansilla moved from Guatemala City to Canada with his wife and twenty dollars in his pocket.

In the decades since, he has built several companies that have employed hundreds and won honors, including the Canadian Business Excellence Award in 2018, 2019, and 2020, along with the AI award of the Most Innovative High-Tech Enterprise Software Company in 2020.

For what it is worth, his team also built the platform for BrEpic Network, which is seamless, and it is so easy to use that a tech lackey like me can quickly grasp it.

David attended the BrEpic Network launch party before Mark Fujiwara and I had the official platform built or had selected the company to do it. Mark, who makes all the backstage decisions, quickly realized that David and his team were the perfect fit as we matched the same mindset and the right collaborative visions.

At the launch event, David also trumpeted the notion, "The observer creates his own reality."

David essentially was penniless when arriving in a foreign land, yet through hard work, learning, and leading, he built an entrepreneurial set of companies. He and his firms also support more than seventy children in his native Guatemala with education and meals daily.

I have a PR client in the healthcare space who moved with his father from Burma—yes, Burma—to Hong Kong with ten dollars to their names. They launched, grew, and sold three eight-figure businesses.

Another partner arrived in the United States from Egypt when he was eighteen. He was fired from his first job at McDonald's and then he founded one of America's top life insurance planning businesses for advisors and their high net-worth clients.

Another PR partner, former Army officer and football player, Greg Washington, walked 1,800 miles over several months in 2021 from Mississippi to West Point Military Academy in New York to raise awareness for military suicides and PTSD.

These leaders observed and created their own realities.

Besides seeing my family, most of my Mondays through Fridays are spent observing the behaviors of top entrepreneurs. They help me create my reality by providing almost all of the ideas and also sharing the potential pitfalls of this life.

It has been incredibly fascinating that my reality—defined

as "the world or the state of things as they actually exist, as opposed to an idealistic or notional idea of them"—has evolved through a mostly virtual world. In fact, virtual connectivity has created real opportunities and significant commerce.

Whether you want to become a multimillionaire or just better your life, it is as simple as observing...but then having the courage to materialize your own reality.

EPIC TAKEAWAYS

Observe, then act.

Do you have the courage to create your own reality?

The virtual world provides endless opportunities for real progress.

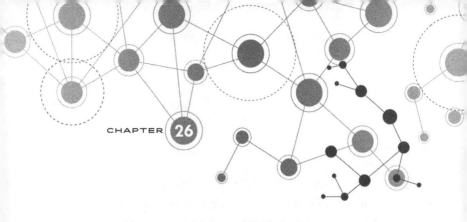

CHAPTER **26**

BE THE BUYER

The Hall of Famer was incredulous.

He could not believe what I was saying.

He could not fathom that people would meet me and within a few minutes want to sign with my PR firm.

I told him it happened all the time.

He was flummoxed, but then he went on to say how great he was, how *he* was the Hall of Famer. He yelled that he would not pay a dime until there were some tangible results achieved. He huffed and puffed that I needed to prove myself to him.

I told him that I needed to do no such thing, because I was the buyer. Companies invest in and pay my firms, but I am just the buyer of the people I want to partner with. I do not sell anything. And everything is paid in full, upfront. No exceptions. No negotiation. Period.

My firms just solve partners' problems getting in front of the media and being connected to the right-fit abundant visionaries. And the right visionaries will gladly pay to solve their pain points quickly and effectively.

As background, a networking friend of mine had introduced me to the Hall of Famer, who was going through some major legal trouble. Note: I do not understand or conduct crisis communications. He was seeking PR guidance to mitigate the bad press. As background, anyone who knows anything about sports will know who this person is.

In the forty-five–minute conversation, the Hall of Famer spoke for forty-four minutes and fifteen seconds. In the forty-five seconds during which I talked about my company, I revealed the process, why it worked, and the level of investment involved. He was not interested. But even if he were, I never would have partnered with him.

Later that day, I texted my networking friend and expressed that I appreciated the intro, and that further intros needed to be to people with the exact *opposite* mindset as the Hall of Famer.

Dan Sullivan, the co-founder of Strategic Coach, stresses to "always be the buyer." As Dan writes in his book entitled with the previous phrase: "At a certain point, you are creating so much value that you become sought-after in the marketplace. And that is when you become the buyer. No longer will you take just any opportunity that comes your way. No longer will just any customer or client be worth your time and effort."

Being the buyer is the best place to be.

It is endlessly fun selling nothing, directly stating how you transform lives with purpose, and then having the greatest people on earth invest in your services and networks. It eliminates the stress of outbound gimmicks, clickbait garbage and funnels, and the annoyance of wrong-fit clients. You only attract right-fit partners, and you repel everything else.

Buyers respect other buyers. I have found they do not like sellers, just as high achievers do not like mediocre people.

I became a buyer by going through this four-step formula I have seen time and time again when people start businesses:

1. Get to get—I reached out to five thousand people to find my first five clients.
2. Get to give—You are starting to give a little but mostly still getting.
3. Give to get—You are mostly giving with a goal of still getting a little back.
4. Give to give, but only to the people who get it.

I think most business owners—and people in general—stop at steps one or two. Maybe they reach step three and never even think about step four. They are giving but always with a motive to get something in return.

I have found the true, pure, global entrepreneurs have attained step four—constantly giving—but only to the people who get it, like them, and thus have become the buyers. Because they get it.

I am truly hoping there is an even more evolved step five out there. If someone already knows it, please provide the details.

Flipping the script from selling to buying will change the game for you and your companies.

By selling nothing and solving real problems, you become a buyer for life.

EPIC TAKEAWAYS

Buying is much better than selling.

Give to give, but only to the people who get it.

When you create endless value, you become the buyer.

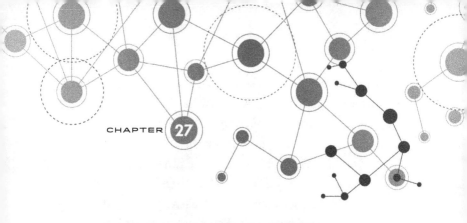

CHAPTER 27

THE TRIPLE WIN

A *Baseball Reference* report determined that from 2001–2020, there were 831,932 base hits in Major League Baseball, and only 17,086 of those hits were triples.

That is just 2.05 percent of hits—the rarest hit in baseball—much more difficult than a home run, which accounted for more than 12 percent of the overall hits.

I have always been fascinated by triples—whether they are three-baggers, triple plays on defense, or Triple Crowns in horse racing—because they are so hard to complete.

I was a sports reporter and editor for the first fifteen years of my career as a professional journalist, so I have always seen the connection between games and entrepreneurship. There is glory, dedication, incredibly hard work, teams, leaders, winners, obstacles, and so many other factors in both worlds.

The rarity of triples in sports and business intersected late in 2021 when I had a meeting with Peter Kofod, a critical infrastructure and blockchain technology entrepreneur and a former major in the US Army. We have become good friends—again, even though we have never met in person—and I would describe him as a genius, literally, because his IQ is 153—well over the 140 mark that is considered the low point of genius levels. I am 139, which I think has been beneficial because I can be a bridge between true geniuses and the rest of society. I can understand people like Peter and translate it to everyone else. As an aside, only 1 percent of the population has an IQ of 140 or above.

In one of our Zoom calls, Peter was noting how most deals between businesses are transactional because there are only two players—someone pays for another's services with nothing else at play. No one else wins.

He stressed that the key for a successful, transformational relationship was creating a "triple win" that, Peter said, "introduces the interests of third-party stakeholders."

"If you include third-party interests, you eliminate so many barriers to growth," Peter said.

I thought about this idea of triple wins and realized that it is why my PR firm had been so successful and why the connecting platform would be even more so.

With PR, my firm wins because someone invests in the service, and I am allowed to function in the purpose of my life. The partner wins because they have numerous opportunities to share their stories with the world through media. And there has always been a third party, which is the media journalist or host, who gets introduced to the PR partner with whom they can create more potential collaborations and connections.

I did a really deep dive into it and determined it is actually a quadruple win because the shows' audiences win as well, since they receive content from the host and "meet" the PR partner through the interview, which enables them the opportunity of potential connectivity.

Dave Young, a true 10–Quick Start visionary who has been a terrific PR partner and was the very first person to sign up for BrEpic Network, described the functions of both as a "double triple win." The wins continue to compound because the interests of third-party stakeholders are always at the forefront, which creates the potential for more and more stakeholders to become involved. It is like a gift that keeps on giving and continues to provide more and more value to everyone involved.

Transactional transforms to transformational. It is no longer a zero-sum game, but a game of endless scoring and abundance.

EPIC TAKEAWAYS

Zero-sum deals create barriers to growth.

Is your business transactional or transformational?

Triple wins introduce the interests of third-party stakeholders.

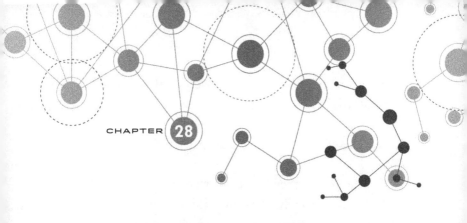

CHAPTER 28

THE SHOOTING

The gunshot victim lay bleeding in the parking lot, pleading, begging, struggling to say anything but..."Help!" and then again, but much more softly..."*help*..."

My wife and I had just pulled into a parking spot in a suburban mall close to our house for lunch. We go to lunch together at least once a week without our sons. I stepped out of the driver's side door and looked behind me where the victim was covered in blood, lying on the ground with his driver's side door fully open. The person next to him was on the other side of the car.

Where I live, there have been only a handful of shootings in my lifetime, but I knew right away that the person on the ground had been shot. Over twenty years as a journalist covering, writing, and editing stories about gunshot victims, it was obvious the person on the pavement had been struck by at least one bullet. From the amount of blood I saw, he would be dead soon if no one responded.

I yelled to the person next to the victim, "HAS YOUR FRIEND BEEN SHOT?"

He hollered, "YES!" and "CALL 911!"

My wife did, and then the person who told us to call 911 got into the car and casually drove away from the scene.

I did not expect that to happen.

Chris Voss—again, the former lead international kidnapping negotiator for the FBI and the foreword writer for my first book—has a great axiom that states: "When the pressure is on, you do not rise to the occasion—you fall to your highest level of preparation."

The shooting provided a real time example of how people react to a true crisis.

My wife, a pediatrician, wanted to immediately help the victim. She started medical school in 2004 and is trained to assist in emergencies. That is her highest level of preparation. She immediately acted like a soldier on the front lines.

But I would not let her do anything other than call 911 because my highest level of preparation was understanding that many times, people with a gun come back to finish the shooting, or there is another shooter in the area acting as backup, if needed.

One of my first childhood memories was as a five-year-old, when after school in kindergarten, my father ran to our car and said his best friend had been fatally shot several times in the head in a hotel parking lot. The shooting was a famous mafia hit. Out of respect for the family, I will not divulge exact details. The person who was shot was featured in several major mainstream movies.

Although my dad was not involved with the mob, he was rightfully worried that he—and his family—could be shot next. So, he tried to hide us in various houses in the area. I do not remember that time, but I ran into a former babysitter a few years ago. She told us how her dad would not let us hide in their house when we came over.

My highest level of preparation was realizing that there could still be a gunman or gunmen in the area, and that I know firsthand victims who were fatally shot in parking lots.

Normally, my wife is the protector, but for once, I was hers in this case.

Most of the people in the parking lot appeared to have zero level of preparation for a shooting, since shootings almost never happen where I live, so they stood idly by. The victim was incredibly lucky as one of the businesses in the mall was a physical therapy center, and the employees were trained in emergency response. They slowed the victim's bleeding before ambulances and police personnel arrived a few minutes later.

I view everything as an opportunity to process and learn, so there were endless lessons from the event. But as a simplifier, here are a few of the best ones.

I. In subsequent media reports, both the shooter and the victim were only nineteen years old. Police reported it was an accidental shooting, and the shooter asked us to call 911 before he left the scene. He was arrested a few minutes later, less than a mile from the scene. The shooter easily could have driven like a maniac out of the parking lot, but he did not. I remember him even signaling to turn left out of the parking lot lane. Based on that, I would not consider the shooter a bad person. Instead, it was just a terrible mistake. It was a chance for him to hopefully learn and evolve.

2. There also was no report from the police or media that the victim died, so I am very thankful my wife called 911 as soon as we arrived at the scene. Although she could not perform her highest level of preparation, without calling 911, I know there is a good chance the victim would have died.

3. People always talk about appreciating your life, and that it can end at any second. Seeing someone nearly die in the supposedly safe suburbs and understanding that my wife and I easily could have been shot—or hit by the car leaving the scene—made me appreciate my family and enjoy life's simple moments even more.

To simplify the life lesson, it really comes down to what you want from life. I choose to be with my family and build my network on a global level. I did not need to witness a shooting in my neighborhood to realize that, but it was a great reminder of why it is important to know what actually matters.

EPIC TAKEAWAYS

What truly matters to you in life?

Everything can be used as a learning experience.

In a true crisis, you fall to your highest level of preparation.

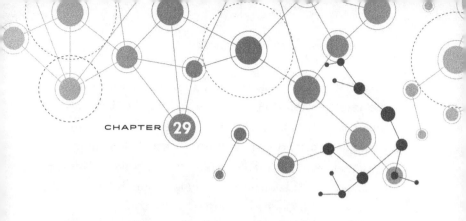

STICKS STICK TOGETHER

The stick story has always stuck in my mind.

I have heard it twice—once in 1989 and again in 2020—told in different ways but with the same moral fabric.

When I was a twelve-year-old in the late '80s, I watched *A Mother's Courage: The Mary Thomas Story.* The made-for-TV film presented the life of Mary Thomas, mother to nine, including her youngest, Isiah Thomas, who would become one of the greatest basketball players ever.

Isiah and his family grew up on Chicago's rough West Side, infested by gangs, drugs, and gun violence. When one of his older brothers left the home for good for the streets, Mary Thomas pulled out a bunch of pencils. She held one and easily broke it in front of Isiah. She then grouped several pencils together and showed her family that they could not be snapped—and that the Thomas clan could not be broken if they stuck together.

Fast forward thirty-one years, and I had a conversation with real estate entrepreneur, Jan Koe, in which we dove into the topic of family first. Jan has been a business leader for more than thirty years. His children are much older than mine, and he shared his affinity for the stick story. He always told his kids to stick together. I remember emailing him later that day with the message "sticks stick together."

My family is inseparable. We do most things together. We love spending time with each other. I know my children will soon have more time and more opportunities outside of home, but they will never be truly away.

My network is the same way. In fact, as it continues to grow, it becomes stronger by the day. Tighter. Better. Even more magnetic.

The sticks transform into an unbreakable bond...a firm force of greatness.

I am a stickler for consistent excellence, and I have found that the greatest abundance can only be found when sticking to your ideals and sticking to your family and network.

The romanticism of the lone wolf in the entrepreneur world is not the long-term answer. Eventually, it will break you because there just are not enough sticks.

EPIC TAKEAWAYS

Sticks stick together.

The lone wolf approach will eventually break you.

Families and networks are unbreakable bonds when working as one.

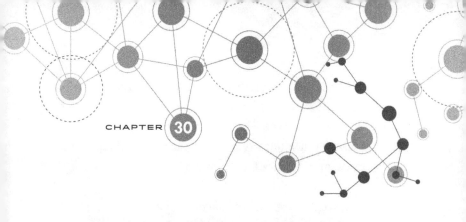

CHAPTER 30

JUST ENJOY PLAYING

I am scribing this chapter on February 10, 2022—exactly five years to the day when my journalist's salary was cut and my entrepreneurial journey began.

I think back to that day in 2017—the feeling of utter hopelessness and panic—to where I am right now: so grateful and excited about the exponentially abundant future. I think about how in five years, with zero business background, I now lead two global companies that only partner with the world's top visionary leaders—or the ones who will do what it takes to get there.

The cream does rise to the top. Thanks, Dad.

The ideas for this book came from a lifetime of learning valuable lessons and then integrating them into my existence. I finished this entire manuscript in sixteen days because the chapters were already there. They just needed to be written.

It is no accident this book was completed on February 10. My wife's wonderful grandmother, Esther, died an hour after I finished. This paragraph was added shortly after I thought I was done. It—was the right reminder of the preciousness of life. My wife is a younger version of her Bubby, filled with love, goodness, and warmth for the world.

Esther loved and appreciated life more than anyone I have ever met. She was meant to be included in these pages.

Godwinks.

I have saved my three top lessons for this last chapter. Two are from famous people. The other, my true favorite, is not.

The number one quote from my number one book comes from *Man's Search for Meaning*—the classic written by Holocaust survivor, Viktor Frankl. In the masterpiece, Frankl discusses how the prisoners who had lost faith in their future were "doomed."

"With his loss of belief in the future, he also lost his spiritual hold; he let himself decline and became subject to mental and physical decay," Frankl wrote. "His faith in the future and his will to live had become paralyzed and his body fell victim to illness."

That is why I, along with any other visionary entrepreneur, am always trying to build a brighter future—for my family, for my network, for the world, for myself. With foundational hopes of something greater in the years to come—and creating the opportunities to achieve those goals, life is always exciting, joyous, and riveting.

Jimmy Valvano never knew that during his legendary "do not give up...do not ever give up" speech at the 1993 ESPYs, that he would be dead from cancer less than two months later.

I think Jimmy V's speech on March 4, 1993 is the greatest of my lifetime not only for what it created—his foundation to help defeat cancer has raised hundreds of millions of dollars—but for the meaning behind it.

"It's so important to know where you are. I know where I am right now. How do you go from where you are to where you want to be? I think you have to have an enthusiasm for life. You have to have a dream, a goal. You have to be willing to work for it," Valvano said.

He concluded: "I just got one last thing; I urge all of you...to spend each day with some laughter and some thought, to get your emotions going. To be enthusiastic every day, and Ralph Waldo Emerson said, 'Nothing great could be accomplished without enthusiasm,' to keep your dreams alive in spite of problems whatever you have. The ability to be able to work hard for your dreams to come true, to become a reality."

Building an Epic Life requires laughing, crying, sharing, and embracing emotions—and most importantly, not making any excuses to achieve your goals. *The ability to be able to work hard for your dreams to come true, to become a reality.*

There are simply no excuses at the highest level...only investment and consistent hard work.

The final lesson comes not from a well-known author or basketball coach but from a teenage soccer player, Xander, who played for our local high school team and helped coach my sons during their summer three-on-three youth league.

Xander is a great kid and a solid soccer player who loves coaching children. He has a zest for life.

My sons and I went to all his high school's playoff games, including his last one—a 1–0, double-overtime defeat in the sectional semifinals. Xander had told me he was not planning to play in college, so I knew the loss would be beyond devastating. His soccer career was over.

After the game, I took my sons to the other side of the stadium where, behind the stands on a practice pitch, Xander's coach was giving the team one last speech about how proud he was of them. It lasted more than thirty minutes.

We waited patiently, passing a soccer ball among the three of us. I wanted my sons to talk to Xander for two reasons:

- I knew he would appreciate seeing them after the most gut-wrenching loss and last game of his career.
- At his rawest, most vulnerable, emotional moment, I thought he would provide life-changing advice to them.

After his coach was done talking, Xander walked over to my sons, who were seven and nine at the time, and told them three key words: "Just enjoy playing."

Of all the great messages from entrepreneurs highlighted in this book, I like Xander's simple sentence the best.

Just...enjoy...playing.

Life is a game to be enjoyed. I have tried to embrace that over the last five years, with all the ups and downs of the entrepreneur world—enjoying every lesson, appreciating every victory, learning something new every single day, and being grateful for every experience.

Please enjoy your life.

And Make It Epic.

EPIC TAKEAWAYS

Just enjoy playing.

Life is a game to be enjoyed.

There are no excuses at the highest level...only investment.

CPSIA information can be obtained
at www.ICGtesting.com
Printed in the USA
JSHW030143080323
38621JS00002B/4

9 781544 532555